LIFE OF CHRIST

the most compelling Life ever lived

C.L. HUETHER

LIFE OF CHRIST

Copyright ©2016 C.L. Huether

ISBN: 1533525056
ISBN-13: 978-1533525055

ABOUT THE AUTHOR

C.L. Huether has taught 7th- and 8th-grade Bible at The King's Academy for 27 years. He has been the Chair of the Bible Department for 14 years. A renowned storyteller, he is beloved by students from throughout his 32 years in education. He is the father of five. He lives with his wife of 31 years in West Palm Beach, Florida.

PROLOGUE

It is well known that many who from the beginning of Jesus' ministry were eyewitnesses and ministers of the Gospel have taken on the challenge to draw up a thorough account of the matters connected with the life of Jesus and those things which He accomplished among us. Since I have searched diligently and gained a full knowledge of those things having to do with Him beginning with the very first events of His life, it seemed good to me also to write them to you in an orderly fashion, your Excellency, Theophilus. I do this so that you will have a more accurate understanding of the trustworthiness of the instruction that you have received about Jesus.

Luke, The Beloved Physician

INTRODUCTION

Eve stood in front of the tree. All around her, as far as the eye could see, in every direction there were trees filling the immense Garden of Eden. God had told her and her husband Adam they could freely eat from any one of those trees. But this was the one forbidden tree. In fact, they had been told that if they disobeyed the command to stay away from here and took of that fruit they would surely die that very day.

But the serpent told her something different. He said, "You will not surely die. God knows that the day you eat it, your eyes will be opened, and you'll be like God, knowing good and evil."

Well, the fruit didn't look poisonous. In fact it looked like it would be delicious like all the rest of the fruit in the garden. Along with this, she would become just like God. When she reached out and carefully touched it, nothing strange happened. So she took a bite and then gave some to her husband. It was only after partaking of the fruit that anything happened, but it was not what she expected. Their eyes were opened but they didn't become like God; all they realized was that they were naked. So they sewed some fig leaves together and made coverings for themselves.

Later in the day, when the sun began to go down, they heard the sound of the Lord God walking in the Garden and they were frightened. Each day He would come at this time and spend time with them and they so enjoyed His company. But today things had changed and they were frightened because they had disobeyed the one command God had given them.

God began to call out to them and finally Adam responded. "I heard your voice in the Garden and I was afraid because I was naked; and I hid myself."

At this point God let them know He was aware of their sin,

and Adam blamed Eve for the incident. She in turn blamed the serpent, but they were all to bear the consequences. After pronouncing judgment on the serpent, God spoke to the couple.

"Eve, I will greatly multiply your sorrow and your conception; in pain you shall bring forth children; your desire shall be for your husband, and he shall rule over you.

Adam, because you listened to your wife instead of Me, the ground is cursed for your sake. In toil you shall eat of it all the days of your life. Both thorns and thistles it shall bring forth for you, and you shall eat the herb of the field.

In the sweat of your face you shall eat bread till you return to the ground, for out of it you were taken; for dust you are, and to dust you shall return."

The situation could not have looked bleaker as they were confronted with God's promised judgments. But then God spoke to the serpent and they heard words of hope. There was never before any mention of the possibility of forgiveness. But they heard Him say to the serpent:

"I will put enmity between you and the woman, and between your seed and her Seed; He shall bruise your head and you shall bruise His heel."

God was someday going to send someone to undo what satan had caused. And so the wait for the Messiah began. The day would come when a Savior would be sent.

CHAPTER 1

Jerusalem was the Holy City, and the Temple there was the most sacred place of all. It had been built by Herod the Great who had been decreed to be king by the Roman Senate on the recommendation of Antony and Octavius. He had become world famous for his ambitious building projects. Since he was partially Edomite, this made him the first king of Judaea not of pure Jewish descent, which was exactly what Jacob prophesied in the book of Genesis would happen when Shiloh (or the Messiah) was to come.

The elderly priest, Zacharias, walked up the steps of the Temple, accompanied by two assistants, towards the Holy Place to administer the incense of the evening sacrifice. Since every direct descendant of Israel's first High Priest, Aaron, was automatically a priest, with the eldest son being the current High Priest, there were more than 20,000 who actually ministered in the Temple. This mass of priests was divided into twenty-four courses, with his being the course of Abijah. Each group served for eight days, from one Sabbath to the next, once every six months, with the entire course of almost 1,000 priests on duty on the Sabbath.

On the various feast days any priest might come up for ministry, and on the feasts of Passover, Pentecost, and Tabernacles, all of the courses were required to attend.

Because of the vast amount of members in each course, they would cast lots to decide who would be given certain responsibilities. He himself had waited his whole life for an opportunity like this one and knew that it was truly a once in a lifetime experience. He was also aware that some priests would never have this privilege. What he was not aware of was that his life, and indeed all of human history, was about to be changed forever.

He was married to a woman named Elisabeth, who was herself the daughter of a priest. Her name meant "Worshipper of God," and was actually the name of the wife of Aaron, Israel's first High Priest.

While a priest was required to marry an Israelite virgin, it did not necessarily have to be one from a priestly family, so it was believed that there was a special blessing for those who did.

Zacharias and Elisabeth had served God faithfully all their long lives. Everyone who was acquainted with them knew that their desire was always to please God, even if no one else did. Each day they kept God's moral Laws as well as the ceremonial rites.

This made it even more difficult to understand the one tragedy in their lives that was an ongoing sadness- no children. Elisabeth, unfortunately, had been unable to become pregnant, and now that she and her husband had reached this age, there was no hope of them ever having a child. They had prayed for years that God would open Elisabeth's womb, but the requests had gone unanswered.

But a son was not the only blessing they were waiting for from God. Along with the rest of Israel, they had been watching for the Messiah, Who had been promised thousands of years before. The wait had begun with an announcement by God Himself to Adam and Eve. All through the Old Testament, more and more of these prophecies came forth through different people in various circumstances. Isaiah 7:14 told that He would be born of a virgin.

Micah 5:2 predicted His birth would take place in Bethlehem. Psalm 22 pictured His death by crucifixion, hundreds of years before that horrible form of execution existed, or the Roman Empire that invented it. Along with these were dozens and dozens of others.

After the Book of the prophet Malachi, the last book of the Old Testament, there was- nothing. For 400 years there was no real word from God. During that time there were few prophets or prophetesses, the priesthood was basically corrupt, and God seemed to go silent. But the prophecies remained, and the people of Israel continued to wait.

But now the "fullness of time" had come, and God's plan of salvation was about to be put into motion.

As the three men entered the Holy Place in the Temple, they approached the Altar of Incense. The assistants lit the coals in the censer, and then withdrew to join the multitude waiting outside, leaving Zacharias alone. But not for long. He froze when an angel suddenly appeared on the right side of the altar which stood between the Golden Candlesticks and the Table of Shewbread.

He was afraid because the Jewish people believed that if there was some kind of sin or other moral flaw in the priest or the people of Israel in general, the priest could die. The elderly priest could surely think of sins in his own life no one else would be aware of. But instead, the first address from Heaven in hundreds of years was to be literally beyond this priest's wildest dreams.

The first words spoken by the angel broke centuries of silence from Heaven. "Don't be afraid, Zacharias, your prayer is heard; and your wife Elisabeth will bear you a son, and you will call his name John. He will bring you joy and gladness, and many will rejoice at his birth. He will be great in the sight of the Lord, and won't drink wine or strong drink. He will also be filled with the Holy Spirit, even from his birth.

And he will turn many of the children of Israel back to the Lord their God. He will also go before Him in the spirit and power of Elijah, 'to turn the hearts of the fathers to the children', and 'the disobedient to the wisdom of the just, to make ready a people for the Lord.'"

Zacharias responded, "What shall be the sign that this will actually happen? I'm an old man; and my wife is aged as well."

"I am Gabriel," Revealing that this messenger was the very same one who spoke to Daniel the prophet hundreds of years earlier.

"I stand in the presence of God, and was sent to speak to you and bring you this good news. Very well; if you want a sign, I will give you one. You will be mute, and unable to speak, until the day these things take place, because you did not believe my words, which will be fulfilled in their own time."

Outside, the expectant crowd, waiting for the priest to appear and pronounce the Biblical benediction from Numbers 6, stood dumbfounded because they couldn't understand why he was taking so long to come out of the sanctuary. This rite of burning incense was done every day, but a priest had never taken this long to finish the duty. He would usually stay only a half hour, and if he took any longer, the people would wonder if he had been slain by God because of sin or some other form of unworthiness.

When Zacharias finally came out, the people were even more shaken. He couldn't explain what had happened in the sanctuary because now he couldn't speak. Because of the signs he kept trying to make, they realized he must have seen some sort of vision.

He finished his week of service at the Temple and returned

home to the hill country of Judaea. Not long after, Elisabeth conceived, and for the next 5 months she kept herself in seclusion.

She explained, "The Lord has blessed me and has now taken away anything people might accuse me of."

In the Old Testament there were couples who were unable to have children because of sin. There were some who may have suspected that Zacharias and Elisabeth weren't as holy and blameless as they appeared, and so God had not blessed them with a child of their own. This would never again be an issue, which made Elisabeth thankful.

CHAPTER 2

During the sixth month of Elisabeth's pregnancy, Gabriel was sent again for the next step in God's plan. But this time he was not merely announcing the birth of an earthly child, but the incarnate Son of God. The announcement of John's coming birth was made in the Temple itself, where news of the incident spread like wildfire. What momentous display of the power of God would be expected this time? But God's ways are not man's ways. This time the same angel was sent to an obscure town named Nazareth, which was considered anything but an honorable town.

Gabriel was being sent to speak to a virgin who lived there, who would literally become the fulfillment of Isaiah 7:14. She was betrothed to a carpenter named Joseph, and her name was Mary.

The Heavenly messenger came in to where Mary was. He announced, "Rejoice, highly favored one, the Lord is with you, and you are blessed among women."

Mary was startled by the sight of the angel, but even more by what he had said. Why would he say that about her?

"Don't be afraid, Mary, for you have found favor with God. And you will become pregnant and bring forth a Son, and will call His Name Jesus. He will be great, and will be called the Son of the Highest; and the Lord God will give Him the throne of His father David. And He will reign over the House of Jacob forever, and there will be no end to His kingdom."

"How can this happen, since I'm not married?"

"The Holy Spirit will come upon you, and the power of the Highest will overshadow you; so that Holy One Who you will give birth to will be called the Son of God."

Then, even though Mary didn't ask for a sign as Zacharias had, Gabriel gave one.

"Now indeed, Elisabeth your relative, has also become pregnant with a son in her old age; and this is now the 6th month of pregnancy for her who was called Barren. For with God nothing will be impossible."

All of creation and eternity now waited for the response of this young virgin. She was being asked to take on a tremendous responsibility. There would be the public stigma of a pregnancy that seemed to be out of wedlock, and the possibility of being stoned to death for the apparent sin of immorality, as well as not knowing how her husband to be would react.

But she stated, "I am the maidservant of the Lord! Let everything be done as you have said."

With that the angel departed.

*   *   *

Mary arrived at the home of Zacharias and Elisabeth. She had hurried off to the hill country of Judea soon after the encounter with the angel. As she entered she called out a greeting to Elisabeth. She then caught her first glimpse of her relative, six months pregnant, and proof of the sign the angel had given. The two women would have a remarkable bond, since both of them would experience a miraculous visitation by God. But there was something even more amazing that Mary was about to experience than merely the sight of her pregnant relative.

As soon as the sound of Mary's voice had reached the ears of Elisabeth, the baby in her womb leaped, and she herself was filled with the Holy Spirit. As she approached Mary, she began to speak in a loud voice.

"You are blessed among women, and blessed is the One in your womb!"

Mary was stunned to realize that somehow Elisabeth knew she was pregnant. But then her amazement grew even greater as her older relative continued.

"But why am I given this privilege that the mother of my Lord has come to see me? For as soon as the sound of your voice reached my ears, the baby leaped in my womb for joy. Blessed is she who believed, for those things which the Lord told her will be fulfilled."

Elisabeth not only knew about the baby, she knew Who the Baby actually was. Only God could have revealed this to her, which meant the world to Mary, who responded:

"My soul magnifies the Lord, and my spirit has rejoiced in God my Savior. For He has noticed the humble state of His maidservant; for, from now on, all generations will call me blessed. For the One Who is mighty has done wonderful things for me, and His Name is holy. And He shows mercy to all those who fear Him from generation to generation.

He has displayed power with His arm and has scattered the proud. He has taken down the mighty from their seats of power, and exalted the simple. He has filled those that are hungry with good things, and He has sent away the rich empty.

He has helped His servant Israel, in remembrance of His mercy, as He said He would to our fathers, to Abraham and to his descendants forever."

Mary stayed at the home of Zacharias and Elisabeth for three months. Her company and help were a true encouragement to the older woman. She left just before the birth of John, and was now noticeably pregnant.

*   *   *

The day came for Elisabeth to have her baby, and it was a boy, just as the angel had said. Everyone seemed interested in the birth of this child, especially because of the supernatural involvement, beginning, of course, with the appearance of the angel Gabriel announcing it. Many friends and loved ones shared the joy of the event because of the mercy God had shown by taking away the shame of being childless from the elderly priest and his wife.

*   *   *

Eight days later, the baby was brought to the synagogue to be circumcised as the Law of Moses required, which would make him part of God's covenant with Abraham, and to be officially named. Normally the honor of naming the baby would belong to the father, but since Zacharias was still unable to speak, friends and relatives took it upon themselves to name the infant. They said that he would be called "Zacharias," since a first-born son would usually be named after his father. To their surprise Elisabeth said, "No, we are going to call him John."

They were shocked by her firmness, and so they pointed out, "Your husband's name is not John, it's Zacharias. In fact, none of your relatives has that name."

To resolve the situation, they finally decided to ask Zacharias himself. They were sure that he would not approve of anything so strange, and would definitely side with them. He asked for a writing tablet and wrote, "His name is John." They were amazed, but they marveled even more by what happened next. For the first time in nine months, the priest was able to speak, and began to praise God. He began to prophesy, but not about the long-awaited son, as all might have expected, but about the even longer awaited Messiah.

"Blessed is the Lord God of Israel, for He has come to redeem His people, and has provided a Savior for us from the family of His servant David; As He spoke through His holy prophets, who have been since the world began, that we should be rescued from our enemies, and from all who hate us, to accomplish the kindness promised to our fathers, and to remember His sacred covenant, the pledge which He swore to our father Abraham; to allow that we, being freed from the hand of our enemies, might serve Him fearlessly, in holiness and blamelessness before Him all our lives."

After he finished announcing the imminent appearance of the coming Messiah, he turned his attention to his newborn gift from God.

"And you, my son, will be called the prophet of the Highest; for you will go ahead of the Lord to prepare His ways, to inform His people that they can have salvation and the forgiveness of sins, because of the tender mercy of our God, from Whom the Dayspring from Heaven has come to us; to provide light to those who are in darkness and the shadow of death, to direct our feet into the way of peace."

Fear came on all the people who lived in that area, and all these amazing words and events were being discussed throughout all the hill country of Judea.

All asked, "What kind of child will this be? The hand of the Lord is definitely with him."

CHAPTER 3

Joseph was confused. He truly loved Mary but he loved God even more, and so he wouldn't be able to marry her, since it appeared she was guilty of a grievous sin. Mary was espoused to Joseph, which was a solemn promise made between two people that they would someday consummate the marriage covenant. It was considered so serious that a betrothal could only be canceled through divorce and, in fact, if one of the partners died, the other would actually be called a widow or widower.

His wife to be had come back from her 3 month visit to the home of Zacharias and Elisabeth, noticeably pregnant. He was shocked since he believed her to be a Godly young lady, but now he had to wonder.

She had tried to tell him about the appearance of an angel, and the promises the Heavenly messenger supposedly gave concerning the Baby. She claimed that the pregnancy was actually the work of the Holy Spirit. But no matter what words she used, or how sincere her pleas were, he could not believe her.

Under Jewish law, Joseph had only two options now that Mary was found pregnant during the betrothal. If he really wanted to show his zeal for God, he could publicly expose her and have her stoned to death, which would require him to throw the first stone. If he didn't want her to be put up to public display, humiliation, and of course, death, there was a second choice, which he eventually decided on. He loved her but he couldn't overlook her sin, and so in the presence of two witnesses he would have to present her with a written certificate of divorce, and she would be forced to leave her home, family, and friends for good, but at least it would save her life.

But he wasn't sure, and so he went to sleep one night with this perplexing situation on his mind. This young carpenter truly wanted to obey God, but it broke his heart to think of not spending the rest of his life with woman he loved so much.

While he slept, an angel sent by God provided the answer.

"Joseph, son of David, don't be afraid to take Mary as your wife, for the child conceived in her is of the Holy Spirit. And she shall give birth to a son, and you will call Him Jesus, because He will save His people from their sins. All this was done to fulfill what was spoken of the Lord by the prophet, saying, 'Behold, a virgin shall be with child, and shall bring forth a Son, and they shall call His Name, Emmanuel, which being interpreted is God with us.'"

He woke up from that dream and now he understood why all of this had happened. That very night he went and found Mary and soon after married her. The only way Joseph wouldn't treat her as a wife was that he wouldn't consummate the marriage until after the birth of the Child. What had been a worst case scenario was now a wonderful blessing, as Mary and Joseph had God's approval to marry. With this wonderful Blessing growing in Mary's womb, they set up house in Nazareth. The only problem was that according to Micah 5:2, the Messiah was to be born in Bethlehem.

*   *   *

God has ways to fulfill His Word that men may not be aware of, as Mary and Joseph were about to discover in a very personal way. Caesar Augustus randomly decided to add a new tax that was to be levied against all those who were ruled by Rome. It required everyone to go back to the villages of their ancestors to actually be registered. All of the family records would be there so that the registration would be much easier. Since Mary and Joseph were Israelites under the rule of Rome, they would be included in this order, which meant they would have to take the 80 mile trip- to Bethlehem.

Mary was already nine months pregnant, so they traveled slowly, allowing her many opportunities to rest. The couple was only 2 of the many who would be journeying to the City of David. As each arrived in the town, they sought shelter in the inns, which gradually began to fill. By the time the weary couple finally arrived, all the available inns were full- and Mary was in labor.

They were desperate to find any kind of shelter. As they franticly searched, someone graciously told them of the inn's stable, which was really nothing more than a cave that stretched out hundreds of feet into the mountainside, and was filled with the many animals that belonged to the tenants. Although it was warm, it was also noisy, and had the strong odor of animals and their manure.

In the midst of this, Mary brought forth her first-born son. She then took the tiny infant and wrapped Him in strips of swaddling clothes.

As far as Joseph was concerned, everything up to this point had gone wrong. Back in Nazareth he had prepared their new home for the birth of their baby. But then came Caesar's decree which forced him to take Mary away and use all their money to make the trip to Bethlehem. And then Mary had gone into labor at the worst possible time, especially because they didn't have any shelter.

And now as he watched, the baby, God's Own Son, Whom he had been given responsibility for, was laid in a manger used to feed animals. What a shame and an embarrassment. But Joseph didn't know that something was happening out in the fields where the shepherds were.

*　　*　　*

It was nightfall as the shepherds were sitting together keeping watch over the sheep destined for sacrifice in the Temple. As they sat faithfully doing their job that night in Bethlehem, suddenly an angel appeared, and the night was lit up by the glory of the Lord. They were terrified.

But the angel said, "Don't be afraid, because I bring you good news of great joy, which is for all people. For today a Savior is born in the City of David, Who is Christ the Lord."

As they listened on in amazement, he told them, "And this is how you will know Him: you will find a baby wrapped in swaddling clothes, lying in a manger."

Suddenly the entire night sky was filled with angels, praising God and proclaiming, "Glory to God in the highest, and on earth peace, and goodwill toward men."

When the angels departed, the shepherds began to discuss among themselves what they should do. The angel had not told them to go and seek out the Savior but why else would they have been given the signs.

"Let's go to Bethlehem right now and see what has come to pass, which the Lord has told us about."

They had an extreme sense of urgency to see what they had been told about for themselves. As they thought through the signs the angel had given, they knew that they were looking for a baby who would be wrapped in swaddling clothes. That described many babies born to the average poor family who lived in Bethlehem.

But not many would be lying in a manger. That meant they must look among animals, because that's where a manger would be.

Mary and Joseph were startled by the sudden arrival of shepherds from the fields, because no one knew they were there. But they were even more amazed when they heard about the angels and the announcements they had made. As they spoke, the visitors looked down and saw the baby lying in the manger. After seeing that what they had been told was true, they went back to the flocks they had left, but as they went, they told everyone they met what they had seen and heard.

In the meanwhile, Mary kept all the things that had happened in her heart, and pondered them.

*   *   *

Eight days passed, and the baby was brought to the synagogue and circumcised, as all Jewish boys were. He was officially named Jesus, as Mary had been told by Gabriel even before conception, and Joseph had been told by an angel in a dream.

*   *   *

For the next few weeks Mary was Levitically unclean, so she went about her household chores and daily business, but she was not allowed to enter the Temple, nor to take part in any religious ceremonies. On the 40th day after the birth of Jesus, Joseph took Mary to the Temple. At the east gate of the Court of the Women, called Nicanor's Gate, a priest sprinkled her with blood, and she was purified.

Then they proceeded to present Jesus to the Lord. First they went to the sanctuary to pay the five shekels it would cost for a pair of turtledoves or pigeons required by the Law of Moses to redeem the infant. Mary entered the Court of the Women and approached the 13 trumpet shaped chests. A man named Simeon looked on.

He was a Godly man who had the Holy Spirit upon him. He had been promised earlier in life that he would not see death until he had beheld the Messiah with his own eyes. That morning he had been led by God to go to the Temple, because the meeting that he had waited for for so long was to occur. When he saw the Holy Family, he knew at once that they were the ones he was sent to see that day.

After watching Mary drop the offering into the third of the 13 trumpet shaped vessels, he asked if he might pray God's blessing on her baby. He took the baby into his arms and began to pray.

"Lord, now you can let Your servant depart in peace, according to Your Word. For my eyes have seen the Savior, which You have prepared for all peoples. He will be a source of revelation to the Gentiles, and the glory of Your people Israel."

Mary and Joseph marveled at what he said, and allowed Simeon to bless them as well. The elderly man then focused his attention on Mary.

"Behold, this Child is meant for the fall and rising of many in Israel, and for a sign who people will speak against. In fact, a sword will pierce through your own soul also. The thoughts of many hearts will be revealed."

An elderly prophetess from the tribe of Asher, named Anna, had been standing nearby, and she heard the wonderful prophecy spoken by Simeon. She was constantly fasting and praying in the Temple day after day. She stepped forward and began to thank God for His unspeakable gift, and to tell others nearby of this blessed newborn.

CHAPTER 4

Jerusalem was stirred when a group of Magi, considered to be the wisest men on earth, arrived in Jerusalem with a military escort. They carried with them some of the costliest gifts of the time- gold, frankincense, and myrrh. They requested to be brought to the King of the Jews, and were escorted to Herod who was the King of Judea.

King Herod was in the final years of his reign over Judea, and was already terminally ill. He was called Herod the Great because of his many ambitious building projects, which included the magnificent Temple in Jerusalem. He was also infamous because of his jealousy and anger, which at times became murderous. He had killed his favorite of nine wives, several of his sons, as well as other family members, when he thought they were a threat to his throne.

All were startled, including the King himself, when the wise men said, "Where is the One Who has been born King of the Jews? For we have seen His star in the east, and so we have come to worship Him."

Judea's Monarch couldn't help but take the situation seriously. If these men were not the wisest of the wise, he could have ignored their words; but the fact that they had travelled hundreds of miles with such valuable gifts, showed they were convinced that this new born King actually existed. Along with this, they claimed to have followed a star, and that meant that there was something possibly even supernatural involved. He needed answers.

He didn't bother gathering the Sanhedrin, which was the political leadership of Israel, since the question he had was theological. Instead, he called for a meeting of the religious leadership and theological scholars. The chief priests came, which included the present High Priest, all his living predecessors, as well as the heads of all the 24 courses of the priesthood. He also included the Scribes in this important conference, since they were the experts in the Old Testament, and the king definitely wanted the men most learned in the Holy Scriptures to attend.

He was only interested in learning one thing from this gathering. Where was the Messiah supposed to be born?

If the birthplace of the Baby did not match up with the Old Testament prophecy, then it would show that the claims about this newborn King were groundless. But if they did match, then he would have to take this threat to his throne even more seriously.

The religious leaders did not even need to search the Scriptures to find the answer for Herod. From memory they recited, "The Messiah is supposed to be born in Bethlehem of Judea, for that is what was written by the prophet: 'But you, Bethlehem, in the land of Judah, are not the least among the rulers of Judah; for out of you shall come a Ruler, Who will shepherd My people Israel'."

What amazed Herod was that what concerned him significantly didn't seem to impact these men at all. The words of the prophet, which they themselves knew, and the Magi who had been led by a star on a journey of hundreds of miles, didn't generate any interest at all from the religious leaders of Israel. He expected that the chief priests and Scribes would have been the first to hurry to Bethlehem, especially since the town was only 5 miles south of where they were.

He didn't tell the religious leaders why he was so interested in knowing the prophesied birthplace of the Messiah.

In public it didn't seem to matter to him about the coming of the Magi or their statements, because he didn't want the Sanhedrin or anyone else to recognize how seriously concerned he really was.

He called for a private audience with the Magi, where he questioned them about the star that had led them. He asked them specifically about when the star had appeared and asked them to be as precise as possible. After gaining as much information as possible from them, he told them that the religious leaders had identified Bethlehem as the place prophesied to be the birthplace of the Messiah. He then gave them special instructions.

"Go and search meticulously for the young Child, and when you have found Him, come back and tell me, so that I may come and worship Him also."

*   *   *

The Magi had come to Jerusalem expecting to find the New-born King in a palace, and now they were on their way to Bethlehem. Although their journey had already been a long one, they didn't intend to turn back without finding the One they were looking for.

The Magi travelled the five miles following the same star that had led them across the desert, until it came to a stop over a humble cottage. They entered, saw the young Child with Mary His mother, and fell on their faces before Him. These men of such wisdom showed profound humility, and worshipped this young One.

These men realized that whenever you approached royalty, you didn't come empty-handed. They had made the journey carrying with them very specific and meaningful gifts. The first gift presented was gold, which was extremely appropriate to give to a king. The second gift was frankincense, which was an incense people burned in a temple to a god. At least one of these Wise Men recognized that this child was no mere human, especially since a star was what led them to Him. The third gift, the most valuable, was myrrh. It was a strange gift for a child, since one of its primary uses was to prepare a body for burial. But for this Child, His whole life was a journey destined to end in death on a Cross.

When they finally left the house, they had to make a decision. Herod had asked them to return and tell him where the Child could be found, because he said he also wanted to come and worship Him. But something caused them to hesitate and think over the situation.

That night as they slept, they received the answer to their dilemma when they were warned by God to go back to their home a different way. They weren't told why, but simply obeyed the Divine command.

Joseph had no idea of the Divine warning given to the Magi, and was unaware of the impending disaster Herod planned, until he received his own warning in a dream.

"Get up at once, take the young Child and His mother, and escape to Egypt. Stay there until I tell you it is safe, because Herod will seek to destroy the young Child."

He wasted no time in waking Mary, preparing the Baby, and leaving for the Land of the Pharaohs.

*   *   *

It also didn't take long for Herod to conclude that the Magi weren't going to return. But what he didn't seem to realize was that it was God Himself he was at war with. When the Scribes told him what the prophecies revealed concerning the birthplace of the Messiah, it should have been obvious that God had a plan. It was not the Wise Men, but God Himself, Who had thwarted his plan.

He reacted in wrath, and extreme anger in the hands of one who has unlimited authority is a frightening thing. In spite of his rage, he was controlled enough to come up with a plan that would hopefully still succeed in eliminating the new born King. He used the one piece of vital information he had gained from the Magi- when they had first seen the star in the east. He assumed, then, that the Child would be under two years old, and so he gave the order to have his soldiers go to Bethlehem, as well as its coastal regions, to kill all boys under the age of two. This would ensure that the new born Messiah would no longer be a threat to him. He didn't know that God had already safely hidden the Baby in Egypt, where He would stay until the death of the murderous king.

*   *   *

It was not long before it was King Herod the Great who experienced death, and as he had promised, the angel appeared again to deliver a message to Joseph in a dream.

"Arise, take the young Child and His mother, and return to the land of Israel, because the ones who sought the young Child's life are dead."

He immediately complied and planned to return to Bethlehem, until he found out who was now the King in Judea. As one of his last deeds, Herod the Great placed his son Archelaus on the throne. Joseph was afraid, because this son was even more cruel and bloody than his father. And so Joseph again receiving instruction from God, returned to Nazareth where he and Mary had originally come from, which was a village with a poor reputation but where they would be safe.

CHAPTER 5

Jesus had turned twelve years old. Up till this point His mother and father had taken the responsibility to teach Him the Scriptures and to raise Him in the fear and the admonition of the Lord. But now, as all Jewish boys, he had celebrated His Bar Mitzvah, which obligated Him to keep the Law of Moses for Himself. He also began to learn carpentry, because, at this same age, He was supposed to learn the trade of His father. He already helped Joseph in his shop, but now He was officially taking up the trade.

Jesus was in Jerusalem with His mother and father to celebrate the Passover. It marked the first for Him, since he now had taken responsibility for Himself before God.

They went through the seven day Feast of Unleavened Bread and then the Passover itself. But now the Feast was over and it was time to leave for home.

Mary and Joseph joined the rest of the caravan for the trip back to Nazareth. The women, including Mary, went ahead, with Joseph and the rest of the men following. They had not seen Jesus, but knew that He was there because they had told Him when they were leaving, and their Son was always obedient.

He was probably with some of the fellow travelers. But by the end of the first day, the now frantic parents had made a complete and thorough search among their friends and loved ones, and hadn't been able to find Him. The last place He had been seen was back in Jerusalem.

They immediately took the day's journey back to the Holy City. They were concerned for His safety because they knew something terrible must have happened, because there was no way He could have disobeyed. They were anxious and fearful, as their only concern was the safe recovery of their Son. They searched everywhere they could think of, and, finally on the third day since they had last seen Him, they found their lost Son in the Temple.

He was on one of the terraces where the rabbis would sit in circles so that they could receive instruction from members of the Sanhedrin. He was sitting on the floor, along with other young scholars, at the feet of the Doctors of the Law. He was listening intently to what was being said so that He could ask good, relevant questions. All sitting nearby were astonished, because His grasp and understanding was far beyond someone of His age. Not only was He asking challenging questions, but also had an amazing ability to answer the questions of the Doctors.

When Mary and Joseph saw Him they were also amazed, but not by His interaction with the teachers, but by the very fact that He was even here. They couldn't make sense of this, because here sat their Son completely safe. This wasn't what they expected.

Mary was the first to speak. "Son, why have you dealt with us this way? Behold, your father and I have sought you sorrowfully."

Jesus responded with His first recorded words, "How is it that you sought Me? Didn't you know I had to be about My Father's business?"

Jesus knew that Joseph wasn't his father, but that God was His Father. The Temple was the only appropriate place he could be to learn His Father's business. Mary had been told years before by the angel Gabriel that her Son would be called the Son of God, but now hearing this from Her Son's very Own lips was astounding. But Jesus departed with them and returned to Nazareth, where He resided until the beginning of His ministry almost two decades later.

CHAPTER 6

It began as a trickle, but had now grown to a steady stream of people all heading towards the Judean wilderness, of all places. The kingdom of Herod the Great had been divided after his death amongst three of his sons- Antipas, Archelaus, and Philip. In Jerusalem, Annas and his son in law Caiaphas represented the religious authority over the priesthood and the Temple. But now John, the son of Zacharias, had appeared at the Jordan River in the Judean wilderness, and people from just about everywhere were going out to him.

He was calling people to a baptism of repentance, which was not all that remarkable. But usually it was Gentiles who were becoming Jewish proselytes, or converts, who were baptized. Instead, John was calling Jews to a baptism of repentance, and was preaching about the Kingdom of Heaven. The Old Testament prophets for centuries had foretold the coming of the Messiah and His kingdom, but John made the startling declaration that that kingdom from heaven was no longer coming- it was here. He proclaimed that in order for a person to become part of Messiah's kingdom, he not only had to be sorry for his sins, but to change, or, repent also, and the response of the people of Israel was overwhelming.

They journeyed out to the wild, desolate district around the mouth of the Jordan where John stayed and preached. It was the Jordan valley, which was the rough region in the hills toward the Jordan River and the Dead Sea. He generally was found on the west bank of the Jordan, although occasionally he did baptize on the east as well, but he was always near the river.

As the people arrived, they got their first glimpse of John, who had come to be known as the Baptist. He wore a garment that was woven out of camels' hair, with a leather girdle. He lived on a diet of dried locusts and wild honey, which could be found in clefts of the rocks which were found all over the wilderness.

People would come out into the Jordan to meet the Baptist. They would make an open, individual confession of sin and their desire to change, and he would then baptize them. The crowds that came out to this deserted place were enormous, and the baptizing was almost continuous.

As the multitudes arrived, John challenged them, "Show a lifestyle that shows that the repentance that you claim is true."

"What should we do then?"

"If someone has two coats, let him give the extra one to someone who has none. And he that has extra food should give some to the hungry."

When the tax collectors asked, he said, "Do not claim from people any more taxes than what they actually owe."

When the soldiers who were assigned to help the tax collectors asked what they should do to show their change of heart, they were told, "Do not use violence to force people to pay more, but be satisfied with your pay."

But he saw among the multitudes many of the Scribes and

Pharisees coming to the baptism, who were considered to be among the religious leaders of the Jewish people.

He thundered, "Descendants of snakes, who warned you to flee from the wrath of God that is about to be poured out at any moment. You also bring forth a change that proves that you are truly repentant. Don't think that you don't need to do that because Abraham is your father."

John then pointed at the stones covering the beach of the Jordan, and said, "God can change these stones into children of Abraham if He wanted to. The axe is positioned at the root of the trees, and God is ready to use it. And every tree that is not producing the fruit God demands will surely be cut down and thrown into the fire."

* * *

As he preached and baptized day after day, the people who were waiting expectantly for the Messiah began to wonder if John was the one they were waiting for.

He said, "There is Someone coming who is mightier than I. As a matter of fact, I'm not even worthy to do the task of a slave to stoop down and unloose His sandals. I have baptized you with water to show that you have repented, but He will baptize you with the Holy Spirit and with fire. His winnowing rake is in His hand. He will go from one side of His threshing floor to the other, separating the wheat from the chaff. He will gather the wheat into His granary, but will burn the chaff with unquenchable fire."

* * *

A solitary figure left the city of Nazareth, and began to make His way towards the Judean wilderness.

* * *

Time went on, and John continued his ministry of baptism, as multitudes came and went. Then one day, Jesus of Nazareth stepped into the Jordan and walked deeper into the water, as He approached John to be baptized. As the two men came face to face, the Baptist protested because the Rabbi from Galilee had no sins to confess, and surely no need for a baptism of repentance. He said, "You don't need to be baptized by me. I'm the one who needs to be baptized by you."

Jesus responded, "Allow this for now, because this will fulfil all righteousness."

So John immersed Jesus in the water of the Jordan. Jesus then came up out of the water, and as he stood praying, He and John saw the Heaven torn open, and then the Holy Spirit descending in the bodily form of a dove, which landed on Him.

And then a voice from Heaven could be heard, which said, "This is My beloved Son in Whom I am well pleased."

As Jesus stepped back onto the shores of the river, He was compelled by the Holy Spirit to travel even further into an area of the Judean wilderness, inhabited only by wild animals. For the next 40 days, He fasted and prayed while the devil tempted. At the end of this extended time, when He was truly hungry, the tempter came once more.

"Do you see this stone?" he asked as he pointed to the round, smooth stone lying there.

"If you are the Son of God, as the voice from Heaven said by the Jordan, than you should be able to turn it into bread."

Christ answered, "It is written, 'Man shall not live by bread alone, but by every word that proceeds out of the mouth of God'."

Unwilling to give up so easily, the tempter brought Jesus to the royal portico of Herod's Temple, which was a magnificent colonnade, running across the entire space from the eastern and western wall. They climbed to the roof at the southeastern angle, where it joined Solomon's porch at the dizzying height of

400 feet above the Kidron Valley.

The devil said to Him, "Jump. Since You're the Son of God, hurl yourself down from here, because it is written, 'He will give His angels charge concerning you; they will hold you up in their hands, so that you won't strike your foot against a stone'."

Jesus replied, "On the other hand, it is also written, 'you shall not test the Lord your God."

Finally, satan took Him up into a lofty mountain, and showed Him all the kingdoms of the world in a moment of time.

"Do you see the glory and magnificence of all this? It's all mine, and I can give it to whoever I want. I will give it all to you. All you have to do is to kneel down before me and worship, and it will all be yours."

"Be gone, satan. The Lord your God is the One to be worshipped, and He is the only One Who should be served."

So the devil left for now, and angels came and began to minister to the Lord Jesus.

CHAPTER 7

At the very same time that the devil was attempting and failing in his temptations of Jesus on the last of His 40 day fast, a group of men arrived on the banks of the Jordan River at Bethabara, where John was baptizing. His popularity and influence had grown to the point where his presence could no longer be ignored, especially since some had begun to wonder if he was the Messiah. The decision had finally been made to come and ask him directly who he was. The committee, which was made up of priests and Levites, had been sent by the Pharisees from Jerusalem.

They bluntly asked him in front of all who were present, "Who are you?"

He openly admitted, "I am not the Messiah."

"Well, then, are you Elijah?"

They asked, because there were some who believed that this Old Testament Prophet would appear just before the Messiah appeared.

"No, I'm not."

"Are you the prophet Moses said would come, who would be like him?"

"No."

"Then who are you? We need to have something to tell the ones who sent us. What do you have to say for yourself?"

John looked at them, finally, and said, "Go back and tell them that I am a voice. Like the prophet Isaiah said, 'I am the voice of one crying in the wilderness; make the way of the Lord straight.' "

They ignored his statement and asked, "Well, if you are not the Messiah, or Elijah, or the prophet Moses spoke of, why are you out here in the wilderness baptizing?"

"I baptize you with water. But there is One standing among you even now Who you don't even seem to know. And even though He is coming after me, He is favored over me. In fact, I am not worthy to unloose the thong of His sandal."

*   *   *

The next day as John was observing the crowd, he saw the familiar face of Jesus of Nazareth, who he had not seen since he baptized Him weeks ago.

"Look! The Lamb of God Who takes away the sin of the world by taking it upon Himself. Do you remember that I told you that there was One coming after me, Who is preferred before me, because He existed before me. That's Him," he said, as he pointed to Jesus.

"There was a time when I didn't recognize who He really was, even though I was sent to baptize so that the chosen people of Israel would know that His time had finally come. But then at His baptism, I actually saw the Holy Spirit descend out of Heaven in the form of a dove and land on Him. As I said, up to that time I hadn't recognized Him for Who He was. But God, Who was the One Who sent me, had told me that the One I saw the Holy Spirit descend and remain on, is the One Who baptizes with the Holy Spirit. I have seen all this with my own eyes, and I declare that this is the Son of God."

Early the next morning, John was standing with two of his disciples, Andrew, and John, one of the sons of Zebedee. And the Baptist looked and saw Jesus walking along, and again proclaimed, "Look! The Lamb of God."

After hearing John, the two disciples followed after Jesus. As Jesus heard the sound of their footsteps, He suddenly turned and faced them.

He studied them for a moment, and then asked, " What are you looking for?"

"Rabbi, where are you staying?"

"Come, and you'll see."

So they went with Him to the place where He was staying, and spent the rest of the day with Him. After spending the time with Jesus, Andrew and John went to find their brothers, so that they could share the exciting news that they had been given.

Andrew was the first to find his brother, Simon, and told him, "We have found the Messiah!"

He then brought him to meet Jesus Himself. As they arrived, the Lord turned His eyes and looked on Simon, and before he could say a word, declared, "You are Simon, the son of Jonas, but you shall be called Cephas, or rock."

The next day, Jesus wanted to go to Galilee; and when he arrived, He found Philip, who was from Bethsaida, the same city Peter and Andrew were from. He said to him, "Follow Me, and be one of My disciples."

After this, Philip found Nathanael, and said to him, "We found Him! The One Moses wrote about in the Law, as well as the prophets. He's Jesus, son of Joseph, from Nazareth."

Nathanael responded, "From Nazareth? Can anything good actually come from there?"

Philip answered, "Come and see for yourself."

So Nathanael accompanied Philip to meet this Man from

Nazareth, and as Jesus saw him coming, He said, "Look, one who is a true Israelite. There is not even a hint of dishonesty in him."

Nathanael asked, "How do you know anything about what I'm like?"

The Lord said, "Before Philip found you under the fig tree where you had gone to pray, I saw you."

Nathanael said, "Rabbi, you are the Son of God and the King of Israel."

Jesus responded, "Do you believe just because I said that I saw you under the fig tree? You are going to see far greater things than these. I assure you that you are going to see Heaven standing opened, and the angels of God ascending and descending upon the Son of Man."

*   *   *

Three days later, Jesus and His disciples were travelling up the road that led to the Sea of Galilee, and on to the city of Cana, located a few miles northeast of Nazareth. To the north and west lay a large plain, while south was a valley with hills beyond, that separated it from Mount Tabor and the plain of Jezreel. They were on their way to join Jesus' mother, Mary, at a wedding to be held there.

When they arrived at the home, the wonderful celebration had already begun. They passed through the courtyard and reached the covered gallery, which led to a large reception room. The servants moved about among the guests in the beautifully decorated room, with water pots for purification carefully arranged for the washing of hands and vessels. Over the days that followed, everyone enjoyed the delicious food and drinks. But in the midst of the festivities, they ran out of wine.

Mary approached Jesus and quietly informed Him, "They don't have any wine."

Jesus responded, "Madam, what does that have to do with

you and me. My hour has not yet come."

Mary called some of the servants over and said to them, "Whatever He tells you to do, don't give it a second thought. Simply do it."

Nearby stood six stone water pots that each held up to 27 gallons of water each. They were normally used for purification, but Jesus said, "Fill those water pots up to the very top with water right away."

As Mary had advised them, they did exactly what He told them to do.

After filling them completely, He told them, "Draw some out, and take it to the one in charge of the marriage feast."

They did so, bringing it to the ruler of the feast. But it was no longer water. When he tasted the water, which was now wine, he didn't know where it had come from. He knew he hadn't gotten it, and so he assumed that the bridegroom had solved the dilemma by finding wine from somewhere else.

He said to him, "Usually people put out the good wine first, and then after everyone has had plenty to drink, they bring out what isn't as good. But you saved the good wine until now."

His disciples had witnessed this first miracle of Jesus, which showed them His glory, and caused their faith to begin to grow.

After the wedding, Jesus, Mary, His brothers, and disciples travelled down to Capernaum, which lay on the northwest shore of the lake of Gennesaret, only 2 miles from where the Jordan emptied into it. It was made even more beautiful with Mount Hermon looming to the north. There they stayed enjoying each other's company, but only for a few days because the Feast of the Passover was soon to be observed.

CHAPTER 8

Jesus arrived at Jerusalem for the celebration of the Passover, and immediately made His way to the Temple. He came to the Royal Porch with which King Herod had surrounded the Temple with multiple rows of marble columns supporting the roof. He continued on till He reached the south side.

This was the largest portion, which was made up of four rows of columns, and covered an area 607 feet long and 74 feet wide. Under its cover, which was the main entrance to the Temple complex, was the Court of the Gentiles, where the Temple Market was. This made it one of the most crowded places in the entire Temple at Passover.

People would come here for inspection of animals they had brought for sacrifice. Others had come to buy overpriced sacrifices, and still others had brought their temple tax money, which had to be paid by using Temple currency, which they could only get at the tables of the money changers, who also required outrageous exchange rates.

When Jesus entered, He saw those selling animals for sacrifice seated in the outer court of the Temple, along with the money changers seated at their tables. He grabbed a number of small cords and made Himself a scourge, and began to run throughout the Temple driving them all out, along with the sheep and oxen. He threw over the tables, pouring out the money changer's coins onto the floor.

He said to those who were selling the doves, "Take these things out of here now, and stop making My Father's House a market place."

The Jews who made money from the market answered, "What miracle will you show us, since you're doing these things."

He replied, "Destroy this Temple, and in three days I will raise it up."

"It took 46 years to build this sanctuary, and you say you will raise it up in three days?"

They didn't realize He meant His own body.

Even though Jesus refused to provide the sign the religious leaders requested, He performed many miracles in front of the common people, which caused them to believe He was the Messiah. Sadly, it wasn't a real heart commitment to Him and so He didn't entrust Himself to them, because He knew what man was really like. No one had to tell Him this, because He had learned this from His own experience.

But at the same time, there were a few He did reveal Himself to.

*   *   *

Nicodemus passed through the darkened streets of Jerusalem. He was a Pharisee, a member of the Sanhedrin, and considered by many to be the Teacher of Israel. But here he was secretly making his way to speak to Jesus from Nazareth. This young, untrained Rabbi, a Galilean no less, must be a teacher from God. He couldn't deny the signs that were being done, which could only have the power of God as their source. So he decided to go to find out for himself, but at nightfall, so that his fellow Jewish leaders wouldn't know, and also to protect himself from the possibility that his conclusion about Jesus might be wrong.

When he arrived, he was taken to where Jesus was, and without hesitation stated, "Rabbi, we're positive that you are a teacher who has come from God Himself, because no one could do the miracles that you are doing unless God was with Him."

Then he paused. What kind of message would a teacher, whose ministry God had confirmed with such signs, bring?

Jesus said, "I assure you, except a man is born again, he cannot see the Kingdom of God."

Nicodemus replied, "How is a man able to be born, if he is already an old man. He's not able to climb back into his mother's womb, is he?"

"I assure you, unless a person is born of water and of the Spirit, he cannot enter the Kingdom of God. That which is born of the flesh is flesh. And that which is born of the Spirit, is spirit.

Don't marvel that I said to you that you have to be born again. The wind blows where it desires to blow. You can hear its sound, but you don't know where it's coming from, or where it's going. That is the way it is for everyone that is born of the Spirit."

Nicodemus exclaimed, "How can these things be?"

Jesus answered, "You're the Teacher of Israel, and you don't know these things? I assure you, we know what we are talking about, and we are bearing testimony of what we have seen, and yet you don't receive our witness.

Since I have told you about things that have to do with the earth, and you don't believe it, what are the chances that if I tell you things about Heaven, that you will believe that? And no one has ascended into Heaven, except the Son of Man who came down from Heaven. And just as Moses lifted up the serpent in the wilderness, the Son of Man has to be lifted up; for God so loved the world, that He gave His only begotten Son, that whoever believes in Him shall not perish, but have everlasting life. For God didn't send His Son into the world to condemn it, but that the world might be saved through Him.

He who places his trust in Him is not condemned, but he who doesn't believe is condemned already, because he has not placed his trust in the Name of the only begotten Son of God. And this is the charge, that light has come and is actually here in the world, and men loved darkness rather than light, because they are always doing deeds that are evil. For everyone who practices evil things hates the light, and doesn't approach it, so that his works won't be rebuked. But he who makes a habit of doing the true deeds comes to the light, so that his works can be clearly shown to have been produced by the power of God."

*   *   *

After leaving Jerusalem, Jesus and His disciples came into Judea, where He stayed and baptized people. John was also baptizing in Aenon near Salim, because there was a great deal of water there. People kept on coming, and as they did they were baptized.

Some of John's disciples came to him and asked, "Rabbi, look at the One Who was with you across the Jordan, who you bore witness to. He is baptizing also, and all are going to Him."

John said, "A man is not able to receive even one thing unless it is given to him from Heaven. You yourselves can bear witness that I said that I am not the Messiah, but that I have been sent before Him. He who has the bride is the bridegroom. But the friend of the bridegroom, who is the one who brings bride and groom together, stands by and hears him, and rejoices when he hears the voice of the bridegroom. With this, therefore, my joy has been fulfilled. He must increase and I must decrease.

He Who comes from above is above all. He who is of the earth is of earthly origin and nature, and so the source he speaks from is the earth. He Who comes from Heaven is above all. And He bears testimony to what He has seen and heard, but not even one man receives it.

He who receives His testimony has set his seal to this, that God is true, because He Whom God has sent speaks the words of God, for God has given Him the Spirit immeasurably. The Father loves the Son and has given all things into His hand. The one who places his trust in the Son has everlasting life. But he who refuses to be persuaded shall not see life, but the wrath of God abides on him."

As John continued to baptize just a few miles from the border of Samaria and Galilee, he began to rebuke Herod Antipas, who was tetrarch in Galilee. He spoke out about the fact that it was wrong for him to have Herodias, who was the wife of his brother Philip, and all the other evil things the king did. Antipas finally imprisoned the Baptist.

Jesus learned that the Pharisees heard that He was making and baptizing even more than John, although it was His disciples who were actually doing the baptizing. But when it was heard that John had been delivered up to prison, Jesus withdrew into Galilee.

CHAPTER 9

The typical Jewish person who was travelling from Judea to Galilee would cross the Jordan River, go up the eastern side of the river, and travel north until they finally would cross back over to Galilee. The reason for such a roundabout route was to avoid any contact at all with Samaria, because of the hatred Jews and Samaritans had for each other. But Jesus needed to go directly through Samaria.

He travelled north directly into Samaria towards the Twin Mountains of Gerizim and Mount Ebal. After walking 20 miles, they closed in on the town of Sychar. Travelling up the olive shaded road, they reached a fork where they found Jacob's well. It was called this because it had been bought by that great Jewish Patriarch, who then left it to his son Joseph while on his deathbed.

The disciples went off into the city to buy food in the market place, leaving Jesus to rest. In the heat of the midday, Jesus, exhausted from the long walk, sat down on the curbstone of the well. He was sitting there when a Samaritan woman arrived to draw water. She was taken by surprise when this stranger, obviously Jewish, said, "Could you please give me a drink."

"How is it that you, a Jewish man, would ask for a drink from me, a Samaritan woman, because our peoples don't have friendly relations with each other?"

"If you knew the gift God is giving you, and Who it is that is asking you for a drink, you would be the one asking Him, and He would have given you living water."

"Sir, you don't have anything to draw with, and the well is deep," she said, pointing out its depth of more than 100 feet.

"Where are you going to get this living water from? Surely you're not greater than our father Jacob, who gave us this well; and he, his sons, and his cattle drank from it."

Jesus pointed at the well, and replied, "Everyone who comes to this well will get thirsty again. But whoever takes a drink of the water which I shall give him shall never, ever thirst again. In fact that water which I give him will become a spring of living water gushing up to give eternal life."

"Sir, give me the water you are talking about, so that I won't continue to get thirsty and have to keep coming back here to draw."

"Quickly go get your husband and come back here with him."

"I have no husband."

"You are right when you say that, because you have had five husbands, and the man you're with now is not your husband. So what you said was true."

Startled by his statement, she said, "Sir, I'm beginning to see that you are a prophet."

She motioned toward Mount Gerizim towering over them and said, "Our fathers worshipped in this mountain. You Jews all say people have to worship in Jerusalem."

Jesus said, "Woman, believe Me, the time is coming when you won't worship the Father in this mountain, or in Jerusalem. You, Samaritans, don't know what you worship. We know what we worship, because salvation comes from the Jews. But the hour is coming, and in fact has arrived, when true worshippers will worship the Father in spirit and in truth. Those are the kind of worshippers the Father wants to worship Him. God is a Spirit, and so those who worship Him must do so in spirit and in truth."

The woman finally said, "I'm sure that when the Messiah comes, who is called the Christ, He will make everything known to us."

Jesus said, "I am the Messiah, the One Who is speaking to you right now."

Just then the disciples returned, and marveled because He was talking to a woman, but no one asked, "What do you need? Why are you talking to her?"

The woman abruptly tossed her water pot aside and went off into the city, and said to the men, "Come with me and see someone who told me all that I ever did. Can this be the Christ, the Messiah?"

Then a steady stream of men left the city and proceeded toward Him. In the meanwhile, His disciples were begging Him to eat what they had brought back. But He said, "I have food to eat that you don't know anything about."

The disciples began to ask one another, "No one brought Him anything to eat while we were gone, did they?"

"My food is to do the will of Him Who sent Me, and to get His work done. As you look on these green fields, you might say that there are still four months until harvest."

"But look," He said, as He drew their attention to the Samaritans pouring out of the city towards the well, "lift up your eyes and look at the fields, because they already white with harvest.

Already the one who is reaping is receiving pay, and is gathering fruit which won't perish, but will endure unto life eternal, so that he who is sowing, and he who is reaping, may rejoice at the same time. This shows how true the statement is that one sows and another reaps. I sent you to reap what you did not labor on. Others did the work, and you have entered into the blessed results of their labor."

Many of the Samaritans from that city believed on Jesus, because the woman was saying, "He told me everything I ever did."

So when the Samaritans came to Him, they begged Him to stay, and so he did for two days. Afterward they said to the woman, "Now we believe, not only because of what you said; for we have heard Him for ourselves, and we are positive that this Man is truly the Messiah, and the Savior of the world."

*   *   *

After the days Jesus spent in Sychar, He came into Galilee in the power of the Holy Spirit. His fame spread throughout the whole region, especially from those who had seen all the things he did at the Passover Feast in Jerusalem.

He preached the Gospel of the Kingdom of God, and said, "The time has come. The Kingdom of God is near. Repent of how you used to live and put your faith in the Gospel."

He taught in their synagogues and was glorified by everyone who heard Him.

Jesus came again into Cana where he had turned water into wine. One of the king's officers who lived in Capernaum had a son who was chronically ill. When he heard that Jesus had come from Judea into Galilee, he immediately left his son and travelled the 25 miles to find Him. When he arrived and found Jesus, he begged Him to come down and heal his son, because he was about to die.

Jesus responded, "Unless you see signs and miracles, you just don't believe."

"Sir, please come down before my little boy dies."

"Go on your way; your son lives."

He believed what Jesus said, and so he left and returned

home. As he was travelling, his servants met him and said that his little son was living. He asked them at what hour he began to get better, and they said, "The fever left him yesterday at 7 o'clock."

The father knew that it was during that hour that Jesus said, "Your son is living." So he himself and his whole house believed.

CHAPTER 10

Jesus stood at the lectern in the center of the synagogue in Nazareth, preparing to preach from the Prophets. He had attended this very place of worship regularly since His childhood, but this was the first time He would actually speak. He had arrived earlier as the sun was descending, along with the rest of the residents of the city, as all heard the sound of the blasts of the trumpet from the roof of the house of the minister of the synagogue. He had entered at the south end of the building, and the chief ruler had approached Him and requested that He act as the Shekach Tsffur.

So He had taken His place on an elevated spot in front of the Ark, with the rulers of the synagogue and the other honorable men seated behind Him. He began to pray, "Blessed be Thou, O Lord, King of the world, Who forms the light and created the darkness, Who makes peace, and creates everything; Who in mercy, gives light to the earth, and to those who dwell upon it, and in Thy goodness, day by day, and every day, renews the works of creation. Blessed be the Lord our God for the glory of His handiworks, and for the light-giving lights which He has made for His praise. Selah. Blessed be the Lord our God, Who has formed the lights."

After He had finished another prayer, the Jewish Creed, or "Shema" was recited, followed by additional prayers. Then the benedictions were recited. In the midst of these, more prayers were addressed to God until the congregation pronounced a unanimous "Amen."

The minister of the synagogue then approached the Ark and returned with a roll of the Law. One by one a Priest, a Levite, and five chosen Israelites read from that scroll. This all led up to this moment as Jesus was handed the scroll of the Prophet Isaiah.

As the people silently observed, He unrolled the scroll until He found the place where it was written, "The Spirit of the Lord is upon Me because He has anointed Me to announce good news to the poor, to proclaim release to the captives and recovery of sight to the blind, to set at liberty those who are broken by calamity, and to preach the acceptable year of the Lord."

After He read this portion, He rolled up the scroll, gave it back to the attending minister, and sat down to preach. The eyes of everyone in the synagogue were fastened on Him.

He began by saying to them, "Today the Scripture that I just read has been fulfilled and has been accomplished."

After He had finished preaching, there was a continuous stream of admiration as one spoke to another. But then they began to say to each other, "But isn't this Joseph the Carpenter's Son?"

He replied, "Surely, you'll quote to Me this proverb, 'physician, heal yourself.' Everything we heard that you did in Capernaum, do here in your own country. I assure you no prophet is acknowledged in his own country.

But I tell you the truth, there were many widows in Israel in the days of Elijah, when the heavens were shut up for three years and six months and a great famine was over all the land, but Elijah wasn't sent to any of them, but instead to one in Sarepta, a city of Sidon. And there were many lepers in Israel when Elisha was a prophet, but not one of them was cleansed, except Naaman the Syrian."

All in the synagogue were suddenly filled with rage after hearing these things. In a Jewish house of worship, had He dared to imply that at times God had favored Gentiles over His Own people? They rose up, rushed the Rabbi, and began to push Him out of the building and up the hill the city was built upon. They kept pushing and shoving until they reached a cliff which jutted out 40 feet above the valley below. They planned to hurl Him headlong down the precipice.

But at the last moment, he turned and went on His way, passing right through the midst of them, and ended His first year of ministry by abandoning Nazareth.

*   *   *

He settled down in Capernaum, which is beside the Sea of Galilee in the regions of Zebulon and Naphtali, which was where Simon Peter and Andrew, as well as the Sons of Zebedee lived. They had, of course, already met the Jesus of Nazareth, but had returned to their fishing business before He made His visit to His home town. That was about to change.

*   *   *

An eager crowd was gathered around the Rabbi from Nazareth, as they listened to Him preach the Word of God. He had been backed up to the very shore line of Lake Gennesaret when He spotted two ships moored along the Lake. The fishermen had left the boats and were cleaning the debris that had accumulated in their nets during their long night's work.

He climbed on board Simon's boat and asked if he would put out a little way from the shore, and he agreed. Jesus sat down and continued his teaching to the crowd on the shore.

When He had finished teaching, He said to Simon, "Put out into the deep water, and let down your nets for a catch."

He answered, "Master, we worked all night and we're exhausted, and what's worse- we didn't catch a thing. Nevertheless, if you say so, we'll let down the nets again."

They launched out, arrived in the deep water, and tossed the nets over the side of the boat. As they watched in amazement, fish seemed to come from everywhere and the nets began to fill to the point where they looked like they were going to break. They motioned to their partners on the shore in the other boat to come out and help them. When they got there and began to pile fish into their boat, the catch was so great that their boat began to sink, too. After seeing all this happen, Simon Peter, James and John, and all who were with them, were astonished.

Simon fell at the feet of Jesus and said, "Depart from me, Lord; I'm a sinner."

Jesus replied, "Simon, stop being afraid. From this moment on, the same way you caught all these fish, you will catch men."

When they brought the boats back to shore, James and John left their father, Zebedee, while Peter left everything as well, and they followed Jesus.

*   *   *

On the next Sabbath, Jesus and His disciples entered the synagogue in Capernaum, where Jesus was asked to teach as He had done in Nazareth. As He did, the people present were again completely amazed because He didn't teach like the Scribes, but as One Who had real authority.

But as He finished, a man in the synagogue who was in the power of an unclean spirit screamed out, "Let us alone. What do we have to do with you, Jesus of Nazareth? Have you come to destroy us? I know who you are, the Holy One of God."

Jesus rebuked him, saying, "Shut your mouth and come out of him, now!"

Then the man began to screech, and was sent into convulsions as the demon violently hurled him to the ground right in the middle of them, and then came out of him not injuring him at all.

They were all amazed and terrified, looking questioningly at one another, asking each other, "What new kind of teaching is this? He commands the demons with power and authority- and they obey Him."

The report about what had happened immediately began to spread throughout the region of Galilee.

After the service, Jesus left the synagogue with His disciples and headed towards Simon's house. When they got there, Peter found his mother-in-law in bed burning up with a fever. When they told the Lord, He came into where she was lying. Standing over her, He rebuked the fever which immediately left her, took her by the hand and lifted her up. She then began to prepare food and drink for them all, as the afternoon continued on with them enjoying each other's fellowship.

When the sun began to set, marking the end of the Sabbath, people began to bring those who were ill and demon-possessed from all over Capernaum. There was a constant procession until the entire city was gathered together at the door to Simon's house. Jesus came out, saw the multitude, and began to go from one sick person to the next, laying His hands on them and healing them.

He also cast out many demons by merely saying the word, as they cried out, "You are the Christ, the Son of God."

But He rebuked them and didn't allow them to speak, because they knew Who He was. The night ended when all the different diseases had been healed, and all who had been demon possessed were delivered.

The next morning, the people of Capernaum returned to the

house asking to see Jesus, but He was nowhere to be found. He had left the house that morning while it was still dark, to find a place to pray. The crowds searched for Him everywhere, but it was Simon who finally found Him in a deserted place.

He said, "Everyone is looking for you."

Jesus said, "I have to go out to the other cities nearby, because I've been sent by God to preach there, too."

CHAPTER 11

Jesus went all over Galilee teaching and preaching in their synagogues about the Good News of the Kingdom of God. Everywhere He went he healed every kind of illness and disease imaginable. His fame reached as far as Syria and they brought all those who were afflicted by different kinds of diseases and afflictions, including epileptics and even those who were paralyzed, and He healed them. Those who were demon possessed were also delivered by His power. As this continued, multitudes from Galilee, the ten cities of Decapolis, Jerusalem, Judea, and even from beyond Jordan followed Him.

Jesus entered a certain city and was immediately approached- by a leper! This man was one of those condemned to stay away from everyone except other lepers. If any happened to approach them unknowingly, they were to cry out, "Unclean! Unclean!" But the reports about Jesus had reached even this man's ears. The poor creature fell to his knees, touched his head to the ground, and worshipped.

"Sir, if you have the desire in your heart, you can make me clean."

He had no doubt that Jesus had the power to cleanse him, but would He even care enough to want to.

But then he heard the compassionate voice say, "I want to. Be cleansed," and then felt the touch of the Master's hand.

He was immediately freed from all the effects of the leprosy.

As the man rose to his feet ecstatic with joy, Jesus sternly ordered him, "See to it that you don't tell anyone about what has happened to you. But, go and present yourself as evidence to the priest that you have been cleansed. Then offer the sacrifice Moses commanded for a testimony to your cleansing."

But this man was so excited about the wonderful blessing he had received, he went and proclaimed to everyone he could about what Jesus had done for him, and the news spread like wildfire. Great crowds kept coming from everywhere to hear Him and be healed. But Jesus would at times withdraw into deserted places where He could pray in secret.

*   *   *

Jesus boarded a ship, crossed over the Sea of Galilee, and came to His home city of Capernaum. Soon it was being heard all over the city, "Jesus has come back and is in Simon's house."

Immediately, a crowd gathered to hear Jesus' word that was so large that there was no room for anyone else, not even around the doorway. Among the throng were Scribes, Pharisees, and Doctors of the Law of Moses, who had come from every village of Galilee, Judea, and from Jerusalem. Jesus stood teaching under the covered gallery that surrounded the house.

Up the road came four men who were carrying a man on a pallet who was paralyzed. They wanted to bring the afflicted man to Jesus, Who they knew could and would heal him. But by the time they got there, there was no way to even get near the house because of the crowds. They decided to carry the man up the stairs on the side of the house and onto the roof. Once they were there, they broke up the tiles and began to scoop out the dirt beneath.

Those inside, who had been listening intently to Jesus, were surprised when dirt began to fall on them. They looked up at the light now coming through a hole in the ceiling and watched as a man lying on a pallet was lowered to the floor directly in front of Jesus.

When Jesus saw the faith of the afflicted man and the four who had helped him, He said to the paralytic, "Son, be encouraged, your sins are forgiven."

When they heard this, the Scribes and Pharisees began to say to themselves, "Who does this fellow think He is to blaspheme this way? Only God Himself can forgive sin."

Jesus became fully conscious of what they were thinking.

"Why do you think such evil thoughts? Which is easier to say, 'your sins are forgiven,' or, 'rise up, pick up your pallet and walk home'? But, all right, just so that you know that the Son of Man has power on earth to forgive sins," He said to the paralytic, "rise up, pick up your pallet and go home."

He immediately rose up in front of them all, snatched up what he had been lying on, and went on his way home, glorifying God. Everyone there was filled with fear and amazement.

They glorified God and said, "We have never seen anything like this before."

*   *   *

Jesus went out again by the seashore and, as usual, a crowd came to Him. He was walking along as He taught them, and as He passed Mathew Levi sitting at his desk in the customs office, He stopped, looked at him for a moment, and said, "Come and join me as My disciple."

He arose, abandoning everything and became His disciple.

Soon after, he invited many of his fellow tax collectors, as well as others like them, to a feast he gave in honor of Jesus. So He and His disciples sat and dined with these people, causing the Scribes and Pharisees to silently grumble against Him and His followers.

They said to the disciples, "Why do you and your Master eat and drink with tax collectors and other sinners?"

When Jesus heard them, He responded, "Those who are strong and healthy don't need a doctor, only the ones who are ill. Go and learn what this means, 'I wish for mercy and not sacrifice.' I didn't come to call the righteous, but sinners to repent."

As the reception continued, some of John the Baptist's disciples came to Jesus, and asked, "We and some other followers of John fast often and pray, and so do the disciples of the Pharisees. In fact, we are fasting right now. What about your disciples? Instead of fasting, they are eating and drinking."

Jesus answered, "Can the children of the bride chamber and the friends of the bridegroom mourn and fast while the bridegroom is still with them? As long as He's there, they can't do that. But the day will come when the bridegroom will be taken away, and then they will fast.

No one puts a patch made up of new cloth to fill a hole in an old garment. Because, first of all, he'll ruin a new garment by putting a hole in it to make the patch. And then the new patch will tear away from the old, worn out garment, and the hole will become even worse.

And no man puts new wine into old, worn out wineskins. Otherwise, the new wine will burst the old wineskins, spill out, and ruin the wineskins. New wine is put in new wineskins. No man who has drunk the old wine wants the new, because he says, 'The old is better'."

C.L HUETHER

CHAPTER 12

Jesus arrived in Jerusalem for one of the Jewish feasts. He walked towards the Sheep Market until he came to the Pool of Bethesda, located about 100 yards from the Temple Mount, which was surrounded by five covered porches. He looked around at the multitude lying on the porches. There were the blind, the crippled, and many others whose bodies were just withering. The eyes of each were fixed on the waters of the pool. From time to time an angel descended, stirred the waters, and the first of these poor suffering people to step in was cured of whatever their infirmity was. Because of this, all watched intently, hoping to be the next one. Jesus stood also looking, but not at the pool. He saw a certain man lying there who had been afflicted for 38 years. He approached the man and asked, "Do you want to be made well?"

"Sir, I lay here hoping to see the water stirred, but I don't have anyone to help who might shove me into the water. So while I'm trying to struggle down, another always gets there first."

"Get up, grab your pallet and walk."

Immediately he was healed and did as he was told.

As he was walking, the Jews noticed him, and told him, "This is the Sabbath, and it's not lawful for you to be carrying your bed."

He explained, "The One Who healed me told me to snatch up my pallet and start walking."

They asked him, "Who told you to do that?"

But he didn't know who it was, and couldn't point him out to them, since Jesus had disappeared into the crowd.

Later on, Jesus found the man, and told him, "Look, you have been made whole; but don't sin anymore, or something worse could happen."

Then he left Him and found the Jews, and told them that he now knew Who healed him, and told them Who it was. They went and found Jesus and confronted Him for what He had dared to do on the Sabbath.

Jesus said, "My Father is constantly working right up till now, and so I work also."

When they heard this, the Jews were even more intent on killing Him. Not only had He broken the Sabbath but now He even claimed that God was His Father, which meant He was also claiming deity for Himself.

Jesus continued, "I assure you, the Son isn't able to do anything, unless He sees the Father doing it. For whatever He sees that One do, He does. For the Father loves the Son and is constantly showing Him the things He is doing. And He will show Him even greater works, so that you will marvel. For as the Father raises the dead and makes them alive, the Son also makes those alive who He wants to.

For the Father doesn't judge even one person, but has given judgment entirely to the Son, so that all may honor the Son just as they honor the Father. He that doesn't honor the Son, doesn't honor the Father Who sent Him. I assure you, He who habitually hears My Word, and believes on the One Who sent Me, has eternal life, and shall never come into judgment, but has permanently passed from death into life.

I assure you there is an hour coming which actually has arrived, when the dead shall hear the voice of the Son of God, and all who do shall live. For as the Father has life in Himself, so He also has given the Son to have life in Himself, and has given Him the authority to accomplish judgment, because He is the Son of Man.

Stop marveling at this, because there is coming an hour when all who are in the graves shall hear His voice, and shall come out. Those who did what was good shall come out to a resurrection of life but those who practiced evil things to a resurrection of judgment.

I am not able to do one thing by Myself. As I hear, I judge. And My judgment is just, because I am not seeking My Own will, but the desire of Him Who sent Me. If I alone bear witness of Myself, you say My testimony is not true. There is another Who bears witness of Me, and I know that the testimony He gives about Me is true.

You sent men to John the Baptist, and he bore witness to the Truth. But I am not receiving testimony from man. But these things I am speaking to you so that you might be saved. He was a burning and shining lamp, and you were willing to rejoice for an hour in his light. But I have a greater witness than John. The works that My Father has given Me to finish, which are the very ones I am constantly doing, bear witness to the fact that the Father has sent Me. And the Father Himself, the One Who has sent Me, has borne witness concerning Me.

You have never heard His voice nor seen His form, and you don't have His Word abiding in you, because you do not believe the One Whom He sent. You are constantly searching the Scriptures, because you think you have eternal life in them, and yet those are the ones which testify of Me. And you don't want to come to me, that you might have life.

I do not accept honor from men, and I know from experience that you don't have the love of God. I have come in the Name of My Father, and you don't receive Me. If another comes in his own name, you will receive him. How can you believe, when you are concerned about receiving honor from one another, and not from God? Stop thinking that I will accuse you before My Father. The one who accuses you is Moses, and he is the one you have placed your hope in. For if you had believed in Moses, you would have believed in Me, because he wrote about Me. But since you don't believe his writings, how can you receive My words?"

*　　*　　*

Jesus was journeying from Jerusalem back to Galilee on the first Sabbath after the second day of the Passover, which was when the first ripe sheaf was presented that began the countdown to the Feast of Pentecost. As Jesus was going through a field filled with standing corn, His disciples, who were hungry, began to pluck the ears of corn and rub them in their hands to break them up into smaller pieces to eat.

The Pharisees saw it, and said, "Well, look at that. Why are you all doing what is not lawful to do on the Sabbath?"

Jesus replied, "Haven't you ever read what David did when he and those that were with him were hungry: How he went into the House of God when Abiather was the High Priest? He not only ate some of the Shew Bread, which is lawful only for the priests to eat, but even gave some to those who were with Him. Or, haven't you read in the Law that the priests in the Temple profane the Sabbath, and are guiltless? But I say to you that there is someone greater than the Temple here. But if you had known what is meant by the words, 'I desire mercy and not sacrifice,' you wouldn't have condemned those who are guiltless. For the Sabbath was made for man, not man for the Sabbath."

Jesus continued on into the synagogue. The Pharisees also entered, and met up with some of the Scribes waiting for them there. They had all come to spy on Jesus. They knew that one of the people who attended there was a man whose right hand had been shrunken and withered by disease. As the service went on, Jesus stepped forward to preach. They kept watching to see if He would heal on the Sabbath so that they could formally accuse Him. But Jesus knew what they were thinking.

Jesus said to the man with the withered hand, "Get up and come here."

As all watched, he stepped into the midst of the synagogue.

Then Jesus said to the religious leaders, "Let me ask you something. Is it lawful to do good on the Sabbath Day, or to do evil? To save a life, or to destroy it?"

Jesus looked around about them as they sat in silence. He was angry and grieved by how hard and calloused their hearts were.

Then He said to the man standing before them all, "Stretch out your hand."

As he stretched it out, it was restored to what it once was. The religious leaders were almost beside themselves with rage. When the service ended, the Pharisees left at once and met with the Herodians for a conference about what they might do to Jesus. For the first time, they began to wonder if they might have to destroy Him.

When Christ came to know of it, He withdrew with His disciples to the Sea of Galilee. An exceptionally large crowd from Galilee, Judea, Jerusalem, Idumea, beyond Jordan, and about Tyre and Sidon followed. It was a vast multitude who gathered because they kept hearing about the great things He was doing.

He had instructed His disciples that they should always keep a small boat nearby so that He would not be crushed by the crowd. This was a concern because since He had healed so many, those with diseases kept pressing upon Him with the hopes of touching Him.

And whenever those who had unclean spirits saw Him, they would fall prostrate on the ground before Him, and cry out with a loud voice, "You are the Son of God."

But every time they cried out, He would order them to keep quiet so that they would not make Him known.

*   *   *

In the midst of all that was happening, Jesus went up into a nearby mountain to pray. In fact, He spent all night in prayer to God. The following morning, He called certain disciples that He wanted to join Him. From the group that came up, He appointed twelve to be what He called "apostles". They were chosen to be constantly with Him in order that He could send them out to preach, to have power to heal the sick, and the authority to cast out demons.

The Twelve included Simon, whom He surnamed Peter, and Andrew, his brother; James and John, the sons of Zebedee, whom He surnamed Boanerges, which means "sons of thunder"; Philip and Bartholomew; Matthew and Thomas; James, the son of Alpheus and Simon the Zealot, who was a Canaanite; Thaddaeus and Judas Iscariot, who became a traitor.

Jesus came down with these chosen ones to the plain below. There was a great crowd of His disciples waiting, as well as the multitude of people from all over Judea, Jerusalem, and the sea coast of Tyre and Sidon. They had come to hear Him, be healed, and delivered from unclean spirits that were troubling them. The entire crowd was constantly trying to touch Him because power was going out from Him that healed all that did.

Finally, He went back up into the mountain and found a place to sit down, while His disciples sat down on the ground around Him. He opened His mouth and began to teach them.

"Blessed are the poor in spirit because theirs is the Kingdom of Heaven. Blessed are the ones who mourn because they shall be comforted. Blessed are the meek because they shall inherit the earth. Blessed are the ones who hunger and thirst for righteousness because they shall be filled.

Blessed are the merciful because they shall be shown mercy. Blessed are the pure in heart because they shall see God. Blessed are the peacemakers because they shall be called the children of God.

Blessed are those who are persecuted on account of righteousness because theirs is the Kingdom of Heaven. Blessed are you when men shall hate you, revile you, separate you from their company, persecute you, cast out your name as something evil and, in fact, say all manner of evil against you falsely, on account of Me. Rejoice in that day and leap for joy because your reward in Heaven is great, because that is what was done to the prophets who were before you.

But woe unto you that are rich because you have received your consolation. Woe unto you that are full because you will know what it's like to be hungry. Woe unto you that laugh now because you will mourn and weep. Woe unto you when all men speak well of you, for that is what their fathers did to the false prophets.

You are the salt of the earth. But if the salt loses its spiciness, how do you restore it? Then it's not good for anything, except to be thrown out and trampled underfoot by men.

You are the light of the world. A city cannot be hidden if it is put on top of a mountain. Neither do men light a candle and then place it under a bushel, but instead they put it on a lampstand, where it can give light to all who are in the house. In the same way, let your light shine before men so that they may see your good works, and glorify your Father Who is in Heaven."

CHAPTER 13

Jesus continued, "Don't begin to suppose that I came to destroy the Law and the Prophets. I didn't come to destroy them but to fulfil them. I assure you, until Heaven and earth pass away, not the smallest letter or punctuation mark shall pass away from the Law. Whoever therefore shall break one of the least of the commandments and shall teach men to do so, shall be called the least in the Kingdom of Heaven. But whoever shall do and teach them, this man shall be great in the Kingdom of Heaven. Because I say unto you, that unless your righteousness surpasses the righteousness of the Scribes and Pharisees, you shall not even enter the Kingdom of Heaven.

You heard that it was said by those in times past, you shall not commit murder, and whoever does shall be in danger of judgment. But I say that whoever is angry with his brother without a cause shall be in danger of judgment, and whoever says to his brother, 'you empty head', shall be in danger of the Sanhedrin, but whoever shall say, 'you fool', is in danger of hell.

Therefore, if you bring your gift to the altar of burnt offerings and there you remember that your brother has something against you, leave your gift there and go find your brother. First be reconciled to him and then come back and offer your gift.

If your foe sues you, compromise quickly while you're with him on the road, in case at any time he brings you to the judge, who turns you over to the officer, who throws you into prison. I assure you there is no way you will come out of there until you pay off the last penny.

You have heard that it was said by those in times past, 'you shall not commit adultery.' But I say to you, whoever looks at a woman to lust after her has already committed adultery with her in his heart. And if your right eye causes you to stumble, rip it out and throw it from you, because it is better for you to have one of your members perish, instead of your whole body being thrown into hell. And if your right hand causes you to stumble, cut it off and throw it from you, because it is better for you to have one of your members perish, instead of your whole body being thrown into hell.

And it has been said, 'whoever divorces his wife, let him give her a bill of divorce.' But I say to you that whoever divorces his wife, except in a case of sexual immorality, causes her to commit adultery; and whoever then marries her who has been divorced commits adultery.

Again, you have heard that it was said by those in time past, 'you shall not perjure yourself, but you shall perform the oaths you make to the Lord. But I say to you, Do not put yourself under oath at all, neither by Heaven, because it God's throne; nor by the earth, because it His footstool; neither by Jerusalem, because it is the city of the Great King. Neither put yourself under oath by your head, because you're not able to make one hair white or black. But let your yes be yes, and your no, no; because whatever is more than that is evil.

You have heard that it has been said, 'An eye for an eye and a tooth for a tooth', but I say to you, do not resist evil, but whoever slaps you on the right cheek, turn to him the other also. And if any man wants to sue you to take away your undergarment, let him have your outer garment as well. And he who requisitions your services as a courier for one mile, go two miles with him. Give to the one who asks you for something, and do not turn away from the one who desires to borrow money from you.

You have heard that it has been said, 'You shall love your friend and hate you enemy', but I say to you, love your enemies, and pray for those who despitefully use you and persecute you, so that you may truly be the children of your Father in Heaven. He makes His sun to rise on the evil, and the good, and sends rain on the just, and the unjust. And as you want men to do to you, do the same to them.

For if you love those who love you, what is your reward? Even sinners love those that love them. And if you do good to those who do good to you, what reward do you receive? For sinners do that. And if you only treat your brethren with respect, what more are you doing than others? Don't tax collectors do the same? Therefore be perfect, as your Father in Heaven is perfect."

Jesus then began to explain what real righteousness was like, instead of the hypocrisy of the Scribes and the Pharisees.

"Be careful not to do your charitable deeds before men so that they will be impressed. Otherwise, you have no reward from your Father Who is in Heaven. Therefore, when you do your charitable deeds, don't sound a trumpet before you as the hypocrites do in the synagogues and in the streets, so that they are honored by men. I assure you, they have their reward. But when you do your charitable deeds, do not let your left hand know what your right hand is doing, so that your deeds may be in secret. Then your Father, Who sees in secret, will reward you openly.

And when you pray, do not be like the hypocrites, who love to pray standing in the synagogues and on street corners so that they can be seen by men. I assure you, they have their reward. But when you pray, enter into your secret place, and after closing the door, pray to your Father in secret; and your Father, Who sees in secret, will reward you openly.

Also when you pray, do not repeat the same thing over and over again as the pagans do, because they think they will be heard because of the many words they use. Do not be like them, for your Father knows the things you need before you ask Him. Pray like this: Our Father Who is in Heaven, hallowed be your Name, let Your kingdom come, let Your will be done on earth as it is in Heaven. Give us this day our daily bread, and forgive us our debts as we forgive our debtors. And do not lead us into temptation, but deliver us from evil. For yours is the Kingdom, and the power, and the glory forever, amen. For if you forgive men their trespasses, your Heavenly Father will also forgive you. But if you don't forgive men, neither will your Father forgive your trespasses.

Moreover, whenever you are fasting, stop being like the hypocrites with a sad and gloomy expression, for they mask their faces so that they may act to men as those who are fasting. I assure you, they have their reward. But when you are fasting, anoint your head, and wash your face, so that you do not appear to men to be fasting; and your Father Who sees in secret will reward you openly.

Stop hoarding treasures on earth, where moths and corrosion destroy, and where thieves break in and steal. But amass treasures in Heaven, where neither moth nor corrosion destroy, and where thieves do not break in and steal; for where your treasure is, that's where your heart will be also.

The lamp of the body is the eye. Therefore, if your eye be in single focus, your whole body will be well lit. But if your eye be evil and diseased, your whole body will be full of darkness. If the light which is in you is actually darkness, how great is the darkness. No man can be a slave to two masters; for either he will hate the one and love the other, or else he will embrace the one and loathe the other. You cannot be a slave that obeys God, and at the same time have a passion for accumulating wealth.

On account of this I say to you stop worrying about your life, what you'll eat or what you'll drink, and about your body, what clothes will you put on. Isn't life more than food, and the body more than clothes? Consider the birds of the air. They don't sow or reap or gather into barns: your Heavenly Father feeds them. Aren't you much better than they? Moreover, which of you is able to add an inch to his height by worrying? And why do you worry about clothing? Consider the lilies of the field and how they grow. They don't labor to exhaustion, nor even spin thread. But I say to you, not even Solomon in all his glory dressed himself like one of these. So, if God clothes the grass of the field, which exists today, and tomorrow is burned in the furnace, won't He more readily clothe you, O you of little faith?

Therefore, stop worrying, saying, what shall we eat? Or, what shall we drink? Or, with what shall we be clothed? For these are the very things the pagan Gentiles seek after. Your Heavenly Father knows that you need these things. But seek first the Kingdom of God and His righteousness, and all these things shall be added to you. So, don't start worrying about tomorrow, for the next day will take care of its own things. Each day has enough trouble of its own."

CHAPTER 14

Jesus went on to say: "Stop pronouncing harsh, negative, destructive criticism, so that you don't become the object of the very same kind of harsh criticism. And if you stop condemning, you won't be condemned either. Forgive and you shall be forgiven. Give and it shall be given to you, a good measure that has been pressed down, shaken thoroughly, and running over shall they give into the pouch of your outer garment.

Is a blind person able to lead another blind person? Won't they both fall into a ditch? A student is not above his teacher. But everyone who has been completely prepared shall be like his teacher.

Why do you consider the splinter of wood in your brother's eye, but not the log in your own eye? Or how can you say to your brother, 'Brother, allow me to draw out the splinter from your eye', when you don't even see the log in you own eye? Hypocrite, first cast out the log from your own eye, and then you will see clearly to draw out the splinter from your brother's eye. Do not give the holy things to the dogs, neither throw your pearls before the hogs, lest they trample them under their feet, and then turn and attack, and rip you apart.

Ask continually for something and it shall be given to you. Seek continually and you shall find. Reverently continue to knock, and it shall be opened to you. Everyone who continually asks, receives. And the one who continually seeks, finds; and to everyone who reverently knocks, it will be opened.

What man is there among you, if his son asks for bread, he won't give him a stone, will he? Or if he asks for a fish, he won't give him a snake, will he? If you, then, who are evil, know how to give good gifts to your children, how much more shall your Father Who is in Heaven give good gifts to those who ask Him? Therefore, all things that you want men to do to you, you should be doing to them, for this is the message of the Law and the Prophets.

Enter through the narrow gate: because wide is the gate, and broad is the way, that leads away from life to ruin and misery, and there are many who constantly enter through it. But straight is the gate, and narrow is the road, which leads into life, and there are few that find it.

Beware of false prophets, who come to you wearing clothes made from sheep wool, but inside they are ravenous wolves. By their fruits you will clearly recognize them. People don't gather grapes from bramble bushes, or figs from a prickly wild thistle plant, do they? In the same way, every good tree produces good fruit, but a rotten tree produces fruit which is rotten. A good tree isn't able to produce rotten fruit, neither is a rotten tree able to produce good fruit. Every tree which does not produce good fruit is usually cut down and thrown into the fire. So, then, by their fruits you will definitely recognize them.

Not everyone who says to Me, 'Lord, Lord', shall enter into the Kingdom of Heaven, but whoever consistently does the will of My Father Who is in Heaven. Many shall say to Me in that day, 'Lord, Lord, didn't we prophesy in your Name, and in Your name cast out demons, and in Your Name perform many miracles. Then I will declare publicly, 'I never knew you. Depart from Me, you who work lawlessness.'

Therefore everyone who regularly hears My words, and does them, shall be compared to a wise man, who built his house upon a   rock. And the ferocious rainstorm came down with torrential floods, and the winds blew and beat upon that house; but it didn't fall, since it had been built upon the rock.

And everyone who hears these sayings of mine, and does not consistently do them, shall be compared to a foolish man, who built his house on the sand. And the ferocious rainstorm came down with torrential floods, and the winds blew and beat against that house, and it fell; and its ruin was great."

When Jesus brought these words to a close, a buzz of astonishment ran through the crowd because He taught them as one who possessed authority, and not the way the Scribes did. And as He descended from the mountain, the great crowds followed Him.

*　　*　　*

Jesus journeyed back to Capernaum, and while there He was approached by some of the Jewish elders. They had been sent by the centurion in charge of the Roman troops stationed there. The officer had a slave that was dear to him, who was at the point of death; but he had heard of the man named Jesus. So he had sent these men to come and ask the Rabbi from Nazareth to come and heal his slave.

They said to Him, "This man is worthy to have this done for him because he loves our nation, and even built our synagogue with his own money."

Jesus went with them, and was not very far from the house at all when they were met by some friends of the centurion, who had been sent with a message for Him.

"Sir, don't trouble yourself by coming here, because I'm not worthy to have you come under my roof, and I didn't consider myself worthy to even come to you. But just speak the words, 'Let my servant be healed.' For I understand obedience because I am a man under the authority of others, while at the same time I have soldiers under me. I say to this one, go, and he goes; and to another, come, and he comes; and to my slave, do this, and he does it."

When Christ heard this, He marveled, and turned around and faced the crowd.

"I assure you, I haven't found one person in all Israel with faith as great as this. And I am telling you that many shall come from the east and west to sit down at the banqueting table with Abraham, Isaac, and Jacob in the Kingdom of Heaven. But the children of the Kingdom shall be thrown into outer darkness, where there is weeping and gnashing of teeth."

Jesus turned back and said to those who had been sent, "Go your way and tell the one who sent you, 'As you have believed, let it be done for you.'"

When they returned to the house, they found the slave restored to health.

*   *   *

The next day, He began to travel west with a multitude. He had gone 25 miles, and after passing Endor, He approached the gates of the city of Nain. There the crowd following the Rabbi of Nazareth met another throng of people coming out of the city.

Leading this crowd was a weeping widow with her upper garment torn. She was followed by an open wickerwork bier, containing the remains of her only son. The boy lay with his face turned up and uncovered, his hands folded across his chest. Various friends and relatives took their turns bearing the coffin, and each time they paused, the air filled with screaming, weeping, and other loud expressions of grief.

Jesus and those following Him joined the funeral throng, because to ignore the scene of grief was believed to be a mockery of God Himself. The Lord saw her as she passed by and was moved with compassion by her solitary misery. As he picked up His pace and approached the despairing woman, He said, "Stop weeping."

He then stepped towards the coffin, placed His hand upon the wickerwork, and those who were carrying it came to a halt, causing the entire column of people to come to a standstill. Looking on, they heard Jesus say, "Young man, arise."

The dead boy sat up and began to speak. When Jesus returned him to his mother, great fear fell on all who were there, and they began to glorify God.

"A great prophet has risen amongst us, and God has regarded His people and has come to help them."

Report of this miracle spread throughout all of Judea and the surrounding territory.

CHAPTER 15

As He journeyed on from Nain, Jesus took time to give detailed orders to each of His twelve apostles. When He finished, He departed from there to teach and preach in the various cities of Galilee. The disciples of John the Baptist went to the prison where he was being held and told him all that the Lord was doing. He sent two of those men to Jesus with a message.

"John the Baptist sent us to ask you, 'are you the Coming One, or do we look for another Messiah?'"

Instead of answering, Jesus began to minister as the messengers followed along and observed all He did. He healed many of their diseases, illnesses, and cast out evil spirits, as well as giving many blind people the free gift of their sight. After all of this, Jesus finally answered their question.

"Go and bring back word to John of what you heard and saw. The blind are receiving their sight, the crippled and lame are walking, the lepers are being cleansed, the deaf hear, the dead are being raised, and the poor are being given the Gospel. Blessed is he who is not offended in Me."

As John's messengers went on their way, Jesus turned to the crowds that were there and began to speak to them concerning John.

"What did you go out into the wilderness to see? A reed shaken with the wind? Then what did you go out to see? A man clothed in soft, luxurious clothes? Those who wear gorgeous clothes and live in luxury are found in royal palaces.

Well then why did you go out? To see a prophet? Yes, I say unto you, someone much more than a prophet. Because this is he concerning whom it is written, 'Behold, I send My Messenger ahead of you to make ready your road before you.' I assure you, there has not arisen of those born of women someone greater than John the Baptist, but he who is the most humble in the Kingdom of Heaven is greater than he. Indeed, from the days of John the Baptist until this moment, the Kingdom of Heaven is being taken by storm; and the strong, forceful ones claim it for themselves. For all the prophets and the Law prophesied until John; and if you will receive it, he is Elijah who was to come."

All the people that heard Him, including the tax collectors, declared that they believed that God had sent John to baptize, by allowing him to baptize them. But the Pharisees and the experts in the Old Testament Law rejected the counsel of God for themselves, since they refused to be baptized by him.

But Jesus went on, "But to what shall I compare this generation of men? It's like little children sitting in the marketplaces, and calling out to another group of children, and saying, 'We played the flute for you and you didn't dance, but then we mourned and you didn't weep.' Because John came neither eating bread nor drinking wine, and you say he has a demon. But the Son of Man has come eating and drinking, and you say, 'Look, a man who is a glutton and a wine-bibber, a man who associates with tax-collectors and sinners.' But wisdom is justified by the works of her children."

Then Jesus began to reproach the cities in which most of His miracles and demonstrations of God's power were done, because they didn't repent.

"Woe unto you, Chorazin; woe unto you, Bethsaida; because if the miracles that were done in you had been done in Tyre and Sidon, they would have repented long ago in sackcloth and ashes. But I say unto you, it will be more tolerable for Tyre and Sidon in the Day of Judgment than for you.

And as for you, Capernaum, which think you are exalted up to Heaven, you will be caused to descend to the depths of misery and disgrace in hell itself. If the miracles that were done in you had been done in Sodom, it would have remained till this very day. But I say to you, it will be more tolerable for the Land of Sodom in the Day of Judgment than for you."

At that moment, Jesus said, "I praise you and thank you, Father, Lord of Heaven and earth, because you hid these things from the wise and understanding ones, and revealed them unto babes. Even so, Father, because this was good in Your sight."

Jesus spoke again to His listeners, "All things were delivered to Me by My Father, and no one really knows the Son, except the Father. Neither does anyone really know the Father, except the Son, and whoever the Son wishes to reveal Him to. Come unto Me, all who are weary and exhausted, those who have been loaded down with burdens, and I will give you rest from your labors, and take away your burdens. Take My yoke upon you, and learn from Me, because I am meek and lowly in heart, and you will find rest for your souls; for My yoke is easy, and My burden is light."

*   *   *

Jesus sat in the home of Simon, a Pharisee, preparing to dine at his table. He had entered the city accompanied by the ever present mass, when the invitation had come. It wasn't unusual at all for the leading Pharisee to send this kind of invitation to a well-known teacher, but once He arrived, things did not go as usual. As the Lord entered, no kiss of greeting was given, no anointing oil was massaged into His forehead to cool Him, and even His feet went unwashed. He was completely ignored among the other guests.

As the meal went on, another individual entered the dining room- but this one had not been invited. It was a woman from the city who was known to be a sinner. There were few if any other women in the room since they and the children ate separately from the men, which made her arrival even more noticeable. She had discovered that Jesus was having dinner here, and she had come carrying an alabaster container of fragrant ointment.

As she entered, she saw Him reclining at the table and walked up beside His feet, which were stretched out behind Him. She stood there weeping audibly and some of her tears began to fall on His feet. As she saw this she fell to her knees and began to dry the tears with her hair. She tenderly kissed His feet again and again, and then began to apply the ointment to them.

The other men were shocked, but the Pharisee who had invited Him said to himself, "If this fellow was a prophet, He would know who this woman was who was touching Him. She is a vile sinner."

Jesus said, "Simon, I have something I want to say to you."

"Teacher, go right ahead and say it."

"There was a certain creditor who had two men who owed him money. One owed him 500 pence and the other 50. Since they didn't have the money to repay him, he graciously forgave them both. Which of them will love him more?"

"I assume it would be the one who was forgiven for more."

"Correct."

He then turned to the woman, and said, "Simon, do you see this woman? I entered your home, and you didn't give me water to wash the dust from My feet, but she has washed them with her tears, and wiped them dry with her hair. You didn't give Me a kiss of greeting, but this woman hasn't stopped kissing My feet. And you didn't anoint My head even with ordinary oil, but this woman has anointed My feet with fragrant oil. Wherefore I say to you, her sins, which are many, are forgiven, because she loved much. But to whom little is forgiven, that person loves little."

Jesus then said to her, "Your sins are forgiven. Your faith has saved you. Go in peace."

Those who sat at the table with Him began to say to each other, "Who is this fellow Who even forgives sins?"

*   *   *

As Jesus began the trek back to Capernaum, He went up and down throughout the cities and villages of Galilee, preaching the Good News of the Kingdom of God. The 12 apostles were travelling with Him along with certain women who had been healed from evil spirits and sicknesses. There was Mary Magdalene, from whom seven demons had gone out; Joanna, the wife of Churza, who was Herod's overseer; Susanna, and many others. They provided food and other necessities from their own resources. As they went on ministering, the multitudes returned, and the activity was so constant, and there were so many present that there wasn't even enough time to eat. When Jesus' family and friends in Nazareth heard about this, they were concerned that all this was too much on Him. They were saying, 'He is going out of His mind.' The decision was made that they would go and bring Him back home, even if they had to take Him by force.

*   *   *

In the meanwhile the work went on. They brought to Jesus

one who was possessed by a demon that caused him to be blind and unable to speak. He healed him, and the man was then able to speak and see.

All the people watching were completely astonished, and were asking, "Is it possible that this Man is the Son of David?"

When the Pharisees and the Scribes who came from Jerusalem heard what the people were saying, they knew that they couldn't deny that a miracle had been done. But they began to question where the power came from that enabled Him to do it.

They claimed, "This fellow has Beelzebub, and it's by his power that He is able to cast out demons."

Jesus called them to Him and gave them this illustration: "How is satan able to cast out satan? Every kingdom divided against itself is brought to desolation, or if a house is divided against itself, it shall not stand. Now, assuming that satan is casting out satan, then he is divided against himself. How shall has kingdom stand?

And, again, assuming for the moment that I am casting out demons by the power of Beelzebub, by whom do your sons cast them out? They will be your judges. But since I am casting out demons by the Spirit of God, then the Kingdom of God has come to you. Or how is a person able to enter the house of the strong man and carry off his goods, unless he first binds the strong man? Then he will thoroughly plunder his house. He who is not with Me is against Me, and he who does not gather with Me scatters.

Wherefore I am saying to you, every sin and blasphemy shall be forgiven men, except blasphemy against the Holy Spirit. Whoever speaks a word against the Son of Man, it shall be forgiven. But whoever speaks against the Holy Spirit, it shall not be forgiven him, in this world, nor in the world to come."

He said this because they kept on saying, "He has an unclean spirit."

"Either declare that the tree is good and its fruit good, or declare the tree rotten and its fruit rotten; for a tree is known by its fruit. O generation of vipers, how can you who are evil speak good things?

The good man brings good things out of his good treasure, and the evil man brings evil things out of his evil treasure. Moreover, men shall give an account for every word they say that has no purpose, but is morally useless, on the Day of Judgment. For by your words you will be justified, and by your words you shall be condemned."

Then certain of the Scribes and Pharisees answered, "Teacher, we want to see a miracle that proves Who You are."

"An evil and adulterous generation looks for another miracle. And it will not be given one, except the miracle of Jonah the prophet; for just as he was in the belly of the whale three days and three nights, so shall the Son of Man be in the heart of the earth three days and three nights.

The men of Nineveh shall rise in the judgment with this generation, and condemn it, because they repented at the preaching of Jonah; and, look, a greater than Jonah is here. And the Queen of the South shall rise up in the judgment with this generation, and condemn it, because she came from the ends of the earth to hear Solomon's wisdom; and, look, a greater than Solomon is here.

Now whenever the unclean spirit goes out of a man, he travels through dry places seeking a place of rest, and he doesn't find it. Then he says, 'I will return to the home I came out of', and when he comes, he finds it swept clean, fully decorated but unoccupied. Then he goes and takes with him seven other spirits more evil than himself, and they all enter, making that their home. So the last circumstances of that man turn out to be worse than the first. So shall it also be with this wicked generation."

CHAPTER 16

Mary and her sons finally arrived in Capernaum, with the hopes of taking Jesus back to Nazareth, and away from the crowds, so that He could rest. When they stood outside Peter's house, they found that the reports about the size of the crowds that Jesus had drawn were not exaggerated. There were so many people in and around the house, they couldn't even get in. They asked that word be sent into Jesus, who was sitting encircled by a large crowd.

Some of those present informed Him, "Behold, your mother and brethren are standing outside and would like to speak to You."

He replied, "Who is My mother, and who are my brethren?"

He looked at those who were sitting around Him.

He stretched out His hand toward His disciples, and said, "Behold, My mother and My brethren; My mother and My brothers and sisters are those who hear the Word of God and do it."

Later that day, Jesus came out of the house and went down to the seashore and sat down. Multitudes began to assemble to hear Him teach, until eventually the largest crowd that He had ever spoken to had come. The crowd was so vast that the only way He could continue to minster was to sit down in a boat off the shore.

He taught them many things by using parables.

"Listen up and pay attention. The sower went out to sow seed. As he sowed, some fell by the wayside where it was trampled underfoot and devoured by birds. Other seed fell on ground full of stones, and since it didn't have much earth, it lacked root and had little moisture. It sprang up almost immediately because it wasn't very deep in the soil, but it was burnt up by the sun and withered. Other seed fell into the midst of thorns so they sprang up at the same time, but the thorns completely choked it off and it produced no fruit. And some of the seed fell on good ground, and began to produce thirty to sixty to one hundred times what was planted."

After finishing saying these things, He cried out, "He who has ears to hear, let him hear."

As soon as He was alone, His disciples came to Him and began to question Him.

"Why are you speaking to the crowds in parables? You've never done that before."

"Because you have been given the privilege of knowing the mysteries and hidden truths of the Kingdom of God. For to whoever has, he shall be given more; but to whoever doesn't have, what little he might seem to have shall be taken away.

So I speak to them in parables because while they see they really don't see, and while hearing they don't hear or understand. And the prophecy of Isaiah is fulfilled in them which says, 'By hearing you will hear but not understand. And while you see, you do not perceive, because the heart of this people is hardened, and their ears are hard of hearing, and they have shut their eyes. They have done this just in case they might actually see with their eyes, hear with their ears, understand with their heart, and turn from their evil ways so that I could heal them.' But your eyes are blessed, because they see, and your ears, because they hear. I assure you, many prophets and righteous men passionately wanted to see the things you are seeing but didn't see them, and to hear what you are hearing, but didn't hear them."

Then His disciples asked, "What does the parable mean?"

Jesus responded, "Don't you understand this parable? Then how are you going to understand any other parables I might use?

All right, this is what the parable is about. The sower sows the seed, which represents the Word of God. The seed that fell by the wayside represents someone who hears the Word of God but doesn't understand it. Then immediately the wicked one comes and snatches away what was sown in his heart.

The seed sown upon the shallow soil with the rock layers represents someone who hears the Word, receives it with joy and gladness, and for a while believes. But he has no root in himself, so he only lasts for a time; but when a season of testing, trials, or persecution comes, they become displeased and lose interest.

The seed that was sown in the middle of thorns represents someone who hears the Word of God also. But because of the pressure caused by the worries of life, as well as the deceitfulness of riches and the passionate desire for the pleasures of this life, the Word is choked, and he becomes unfruitful.

But the seed that fell on the good ground represents someone with a good and honest heart who hears the Word of God, understands and holds fast to it, and with patience they bear fruit, and produce 30, 60, or 100 times what was planted.

But no one brings a lamp to put it under some household item, or under a bed, do they? They put it on a lampstand so that all those who enter may see the light. For there is nothing hidden that shall not be made known, or anything concealed which shall not come into full view. So, again, be careful what you hear and how you hear it. Because in the measure by which you are measuring, it will be measured to you, with some added on top of that."

*   *   *

Jesus continued His ministry of teaching the multitude with parables. "The Kingdom of Heaven is as if a man should throw some seed in the earth. He goes on sleeping at night and rising during the day while the seed goes on growing. Finally it sprouts, but he doesn't know how. For the earth bears fruit of itself, first the blade, then the ear, and after that the fully-developed corn in the ear. But when the fruit yields itself, he immediately sends forth those with sickles, because the harvest is ready."

Then He served up another parable, "The Kingdom of Heaven is like a man who sowed good seed in his field. But while men slumbered, his enemy came and sowed tares throughout the wheat, and then left. But when the wheat seed began to produce, the tares began to appear also.

The servants of the master came to him, and said, 'Master, didn't you sow good seed in your field? Where did the tares come from?'

'An enemy has done this.'

'Do you want us to go and collect the tares?'

'No, in case while you're gathering up the tares, you pull up the wheat with it. Allow both to grow together until the harvest, and at that time I will say to the harvesters, 'Gather first the tares and bind them into bundles to be burned, but gather the wheat into my barn.'"

Then Jesus asked, "What is the Kingdom of Heaven like, or by what illustration shall we explain it? It's like a grain of mustard seed, which a man took, and sowed in his field. It is the smallest of all seeds planted in the earth, but when it is full-grown it becomes greater than all of the garden herbs. It grows to the shape and size of a tree which puts out great branches, so that the birds of the air may settle there.

And the Kingdom of Heaven is like yeast, which a woman took and mixed with three measures of wheat flour until all of it was filled with yeast."

Using many parables like these, Jesus spoke the Word of God unto them as they were able to understand. In fact, He didn't speak even one thing to them without using a parable. But in private He made it a habit of fully explaining everything to His disciples. And so when Jesus sent the multitude away and came into the house, His disciples came to Him. "Lord, quickly, explain the parable of the Wheat and the Tares."

"He who sows the good seed is the Son of Man. The field is the world, and the good seed are the children of the Kingdom. But the tares are the children of the wicked one, and the enemy who sowed them is the devil. The harvest is the end of the world; and the harvesters are the angels.

Therefore, as the tares are gathered and burned in the fire, so shall it be in the end of this age. The Son of Man shall send forth His angels, and they shall gather out of His Kingdom all those who create stumbling blocks for others, and those who practice lawlessness, and they shall throw them into the furnace of fire, where there shall be wailing and gnashing of teeth. Then those who are righteous shall shine forth like the sun, when it bursts through the clouds which have hidden it, in the Kingdom of their Father. He who has ears to hear, let him hear.

The Kingdom of Heaven is like a treasure which has been hidden in a field, which, after a man found it, he hid, and because he is so joyful, goes and sells all that he has, and buys that field.

Again, the Kingdom of Heaven is like a travelling merchant seeking beautiful pearls. When he finds one pearl of great value, he goes off and sells all that he has, and buys it in the market place.

Again, the Kingdom of Heaven is like a dragnet which was thrown into the sea and gathered some of every kind of fish. When it was filled, they drew it onto the beach, and sat down and gathered up the good ones into containers, but they threw the worthless away. So shall it be at the end of the age. The angels shall go out and separate those who are evil out of the midst of those who are righteous, and shall throw them into the furnace of fire. There shall be wailing and gnashing of teeth."

Jesus then asked them, "Have you understood all these things?"

They said to Him, "Yes."

Then He concluded, "Because of this, every scribe who is instructed in the teachings of the Kingdom of Heaven is like a man who is the master of a house, who brings out of his treasure house things new, and things that have been used."

CHAPTER 17

That night when Jesus finished these parables He decided to leave that place.

When evening had fully come, He came out of the house and saw a crowd gathering, and said to His disciples, "Let us go over to the other side."

He dismissed the crowd, boarded the ship, and His disciples followed. They put out to sea and, as they sailed, He fell asleep in the stern on a leather cushion.

Suddenly, a storm descended from Mount Hermon through the Jordan Gorge and burst onto the Sea of Galilee. It was a whirlwind of furious gusts that caused everything to shake like an earthquake. The waves beat the boat, eventually covering and hiding it so that it was filling with water. They were in grave danger, but Jesus went on sleeping in the midst of it.

They roused Him up, saying, "Master, don't You care that we are going to die. Save us, quickly."

He looked up at them, and said, "Why are you so fearful, you of little faith?"

He arose to His feet, rebuked the wind, and commanded the raging sea, "Calm down and be still."

There came a great calm.

Then He said to His disciples, "Where is your faith?"

They were terrified, and marveled, saying to one another, "Who is this? He commands the wind and the sea, and they obey Him!"

It was late when they finally reached the shore near the Gergesenes cemetery. What had been a frightening night, so far, was not over yet. As they stepped out of the ship and began to make their way forward, two men rushed out of the darkness and out of the tombs. They had at one time lived in the town but then the demons came, and then they were out of control. The townspeople had often tried to restrain them by chaining their hands and feet. But they would snap the chains in two and crush the shackles. No one had been strong enough to control them.

They had finally made a home among the tombs, where they stayed for a long time. You could hear them night and day screaming and shrieking, while cutting themselves up with stones. They would attack anyone who attempted to pass through that way, and now they threatened Jesus and His disciples. When they saw Him from a distance, they came sprinting. They were naked, demon-possessed, violent, and rushing directly towards them; but instead of attacking, they fell down prostrate before Him in worship.

They cried out, "Do not torment us before the appointed time."

Jesus questioned, "What is your name?"

One of them answered, "Our name is Legion, because there are many of us."

They begged Him not to send them out of the country, nor into the abyss. On a mountain in the distance, a great herd of 2,000 hogs were feeding. The demons begged Jesus to permit them to go into the swine.

Jesus simply said, "Go."

The demons instantly left the man and entered into the hogs. Then one after another the entire herd ran violently headlong down a steep place and drowned in the sea. The ones that were feeding the swine fled into the city and nearby farms, reporting all they had seen, including what had happened to the men who were demon possessed.

The whole city came out to see for themselves what had happened. They saw Jesus, and the men who had been demon possessed, sitting at His feet, clothed, and in their right mind; and they were afraid. Those who had seen everything, dictated in detail what had happened to the two demoniacs, and to the hogs; and they were even more afraid. Thus, the whole multitude from the surrounding territory begged Jesus to leave their area.

When He was climbing back into the boat, the men who had been possessed pleaded with Him for permission to go with Him.

But Jesus sent them away, saying, "Return to your home, and tell your friends and relatives the great things the Lord has done for you because He had sympathy on you."

Not only did they do this but they went off throughout the whole city, as well as the other ten communities round about it, proclaiming openly all the great things Jesus had done for them; and everyone who heard wondered.

*   *   *

The next morning, the boat carrying Jesus and His disciples arrived at Capernaum. He was still by the seashore, and the welcoming throng had already begun to build, and seemed to grow with every step they took. They pressed in and seemed to be in danger of crushing Him when suddenly Jairus, the ruler of the synagogue, fell at His feet in extreme reverence.

He began to beg Jesus, "My only daughter is almost to her last breath. Please come before she dies. Lay your hands on her, and I know she'll live."

The Lord and His disciples trailed Jairus, and by now the crowd was suffocating. Among the countless people was a certain woman who should not have even been there, but she was desperate. She was ceremonially unclean because she was bleeding internally. In fact, she had been in this condition for 12 years, in spite of the fact that she had spent all she had going to doctor after doctor and, worst of all, instead of getting better she had only gotten worse.

But she had heard of this man Who had performed miracles, healed the sick, and even raised the dead. He was her only hope. She had arrived now and could see Him, but because of the overwhelming crowd, and her weakness due to blood loss, she knew she couldn't push through.

So she fell to her knees and began to try to crawl to Him, getting stepped on and kicked as she struggled onward.

She began to realize she would never reach Him, but she said to herself, "If I can just touch His robe, I'll be healed."

She finally got close enough to reach from behind Him and touch the hem of His garment. Immediately she realized the bleeding had stopped, but then Jesus also stopped, turned, and to her horror, she heard Him ask, "Who touched My clothes?"

When all began to deny it, Peter and the rest of the disciples said, "The throng is almost crushing you, and you ask, 'Who touched My clothes?'"

As He was looking from person to person, He replied, "I know someone touched Me, because I felt power go out of Me."

When the woman realized that she couldn't hide what she had done, or what had been done for her, she fell down before Him, trembling with fear, because she knew she had broken the Law by even being there. She explained in front of everyone present why she had touched Him, and how she was immediately healed when she did.

Jesus said to her, "Daughter, take comfort; your faith has made you whole. Go in peace."

As He was speaking, someone arrived from the home of the ruler of the synagogue with a sad message. "There is no reason to bother the Teacher any longer. Your daughter died."

But when Jesus heard this, He replied, "Don't be afraid. Only believe, and your daughter will live again."

As the Master got closer to Jairus' home, the uproar could be heard even outside in the street. Minstrels were playing flutes, and people screamed and wailed with grief.

He entered, accompanied by only Peter, James, and John, and said to those present, "Why are you weeping and wailing? The little girl isn't dead. She's only sleeping."

They began to laugh and mock Christ because they knew the girl had died. So He threw the people out of the home and led His disciples, along with the girl's parents, into where she was lying. He took her by the hand, and said, "Little one, arise." Her spirit returned, and she immediately got up and began to walk around.

The parents stared in astonishment. Jesus charged them sternly that they shouldn't tell anyone about what had happened, and then, that they should give her something to eat. But the report of this incident eventually spread throughout the land.

As they left and travelled up the road, two blind men followed, crying out, "Son of David, Have mercy on us and help us."

When Jesus came into house where He was staying, the blind men were brought to Him, begging Him for their sight. He asked, "Do you believe I'm able to do this?"

They said, "Yes, Master."

Then He touched their eyes, saying, "According to your faith, let it happen to you."

Their eyes were opened and Jesus sternly charged them, "See to it that no one knows about this." But when they left, they blazed abroad His fame throughout the whole land.

Later, they went out again, and a demon possessed man who couldn't speak was brought to Him. When the demon was cast out, the man began to speak, and the crowd of onlookers responded, "We have never seen anything like this in Israel."

But the Pharisees again said, "He casts out demons because He has been given power by the ruler of the demons."

CHAPTER 18

The first place Jesus went to after leaving Capernaum was back to His hometown of Nazareth, this time accompanied by His disciples. The Sabbath Day found Jesus in the synagogue where He was again asked to speak by the ruler of the synagogue. As He taught, the people were completely dumbfounded, and said, "Where did this fellow get this wisdom? How does He perform these miracles? Isn't this the Son of the Carpenter, Who Himself became a carpenter? Isn't His mother named Mary, and His brothers, James, Joses, Jude, and Simon? And aren't all His sisters here with us? Where does He get the power to do all these things?"

They objected to Him, and refused to acknowledge Him for Who He was.

Jesus said, "A prophet is shown honor and due respect everywhere except in His Own country and among His Own people."

He couldn't do even one mighty work and only healed a few

sick people by laying His hands on them. He truly marveled at the unbelief of His Own people.

So He began to go around the other villages surrounding Nazareth, teaching them in their synagogues. He was preaching the Gospel of the Kingdom and healing every sickness, and every disease. But as He saw the multitudes, He was moved with compassion for them because they were exhausted by life's troubles, and literally cast down with despair like sheep who had no shepherd.

Then He said to His disciples, "The harvest is truly great but the laborers are few. Therefore, beg the Lord of the Harvest to thrust out workers quickly into His Harvest."

*   *   *

The time came when Jesus called twelve of His disciples to Him and prepared to send them out two by two. The names of the Apostles, which was what they were now to be called, were first Simon, who is called Peter, and Andrew his brother; James, the son of Zebedee, and John his brother; Philip, and Bartholomew; Thomas, and Matthew the tax collector; James, the son of Alpheus, and Lebbaeus Thaddaeus; Simon the Canaanite, and Judas Iscariot, who betrayed Him.

He gave them power and authority to cast out all demons, and to heal every disease and sickness. He was preparing to send them to heal the sick and preach the Kingdom of God.

"Do not go into the road of the Gentiles or enter into any city of the Samaritans. But go to the sheep of the House of Israel who have lost their way and are wandering with no guide. As you go, preach, and when you do, say, 'The Kingdom of Heaven is almost here.' Heal the sick, raise the dead, cleanse the lepers, and cast out demons. Freely you have received, so freely give."

He commanded them not to take anything for their journey except one walking stick. He explained that they weren't to take gold, silver, or brass in their money belt, or a beggar's bag; no bread or extra coat or sandals, because a workman is worthy of his provisions.

"In whatever city or town you enter, inquire whose home would be suitable. As you are entering the home, pay your respects; and if the house is worthy, let your peace come upon it; but if not, let your peace return to you. Be a guest there until you leave the city. Whatever place will not receive or welcome you or listen to what you have to say, while you are leaving that house or city, shake the very dust off your feet like you would when leaving a heathen city as a witness against them. I assure you it will be more tolerable for the land of Sodom and Gomorrah in the Day of Judgment than for that city.

Behold, I am the One Who is sending you out as sheep in the midst of wolves, so be as cautious as snakes, but as honest and guileless as doves. And be on guard against those men who are like wolves, for they will deliver you up to judicial councils and scourge you in their synagogues. And you shall be brought before governors and even kings on account of Me, which will give you the opportunity to testify to them and the Gentiles. And when they do deliver you up, don't be anxious about how you are to speak or even what you should say, for it will be given to you in that very hour the words you should say. For you are not the ones who will be speaking, but the Spirit of Your Father will be speaking in you.

In fact, a brother shall deliver up a brother to death, and a father a child. Children will rise up against parents and cause them to be put to death. And you shall be hated by all on account of My Name, but he who perseveres to the end shall be saved. But when they persecute you in this city, flee to another, for I assure you, you will not finish the cities of Israel until the Son of Man comes.

A student is not above the teacher, nor a slave above his master. It is enough for the student to be exactly like His teacher and the slave like his master. So since they have called the Master of the house, Beelzebub, how much worse shall they call those of His house?

Don't fear them, for there is not even one thing that is covered up which shall not be uncovered, nor secret which shall not be made known. What I am telling you in private, speak about in public, and what is whispered into your ear, proclaim publicly from the house-tops.

And stop fearing those who can kill the body but don't have the power to kill the soul. But, instead, fear Him Who has the power to bring both body and soul to the everlasting misery of hell. Aren't two little sparrows sold for a penny? Yet not one of them shall fall to the ground against the will of your father. But all the hairs of your head have been counted. So stop being afraid, because you are more valuable than many sparrows.

Therefore, everyone that will confess in front of men that he knows Me, I will confess in front of My Father in Heaven that I know him. But whoever denies before men that he knows Me I will also deny that I know him, in front of My father Who is in Heaven.

Don't think that I came to suddenly cast peace upon the earth. I didn't come to cast peace but a sword. For My coming will turn a man against his father, a daughter against her mother, and a daughter in law against her mother in law. A man's enemies shall be those of his own household. He that loves father or mother more than Me is not worthy of Me, and he who loves son or daughter more than Me is not worthy of Me. He who does not take up his cross and follow up the same road I take is not worthy Me.

He that finds his life shall lose it, and he that loses his life because of Me shall find it. He that receives you receives Me, and he that receives Me receives Him that sent Me. He that receives a prophet in the name of a prophet will receive a prophet's reward, and he that receives a righteous man in the name of a righteous man shall receive a righteous man's reward. And whoever gives a cup of cold water to one of these little ones only in the name of a disciple, I assure you, he will in no way lose his reward."

When Jesus finished giving each of the 12 Apostles their instructions and sent them on their mission, He went out to preach in the cities of Galilee. After the Apostles left, they went out preaching that men should repent and believe the Gospel. They went everywhere casting out demons, and anointing with oil many that were sick, and healing them.

*   *   *

King Herod, who was the tetrarch over Galilee, began to hear reports of what was being done by Jesus and His disciples. But he was at a loss to explain how this man could be doing these mighty works. Some were saying that He was actually Elijah raised from the dead, or maybe one of the other early prophets. But He himself believed that this must be John the Baptist who had risen from the dead, and that was why these miracles were possible.

Herod, himself, had arrested John when the preacher had openly condemned his marriage to Herodias as unlawful because she was actually married to Herod's brother, Philip, who was still alive. He had been placed in the fortress of Machaerus, located on a cliff at the end of a narrow ridge, which was surrounded by deep ravines on the east side of the Dead Sea. On the other end of the ridge stood a great wall with two hundred foot towers on each corner. Inside the enclosure was a magnificent, luxurious palace with windows that allowed someone to look out over the Dead Sea, the Jordan River, and Jerusalem. One hundred fifty yards up on the steep eastern slope stood the citadel where John was kept in an underground dungeon.

John's criticism enraged Herodias, and so he had been arrested, but she wanted more. She wanted him silenced for good. Herod wanted to do away with him also, but he wouldn't allow him to be killed because he recognized that he was a righteous and holy man whom he feared. From time to time he actually enjoyed going down to the dungeon to speak with him. He was also concerned with how the people would react if the Baptist was killed, since they all considered him to be a prophet.

He was kept isolated in that place for almost ten months, while Herodias waited for her opportunity. It finally came. Herod was to celebrate his birthday, and so he invited noblemen, military leaders, and other prominent men from Galilee to join him at the palace fortress. They were all gathered together eating, drinking, and enjoying the banquet when Herodias' daughter entered. The young princess began a lewd and seductive dance in front of all these men, and they loved it.

Herod was especially pleased and, when she had finished, loudly declared, "Go ahead and ask me for anything your heart desires, and I'll give it to you. I swear that you can ask for half my kingdom, and it will be yours."

The girl went to her mother and asked, "What shall I ask for myself?"

Herodias cruelly replied, "The head of John the Baptist."

Her daughter hurried back in, went immediately to the king and informed him, "What I want is for you to give me right here and now, on a platter- the head of John the Baptist."

When Herod heard this and realized what he had done, he became very sorry. But because of the oath he had sworn, and in order to save face in front of the men who were there and had heard it, he gave the order for it to be brought. The executioner was sent to the dungeon, and John the Baptist was beheaded.

The head was then brought on a platter as the girl had demanded, and it was given to her. She then presented it to a very pleased Queen Herodias. When John's disciples heard what had happened, they came, took his body and buried it in a tomb, and then went and informed Jesus.

Remembering all of this, Herod said to his servants, "John, I beheaded. But then who is this I am hearing these reports about?"

From then on, he tried time after time to have the opportunity to see the Rabbi from Nazareth.

CHAPTER 19

Around the time Jesus was told what happened to John, the Apostles returned from their mission trip. They gathered with their Master and told Him about all the things they had done, and what they had taught.

He said to them, "Come apart to a private place, so that you can get some rest."

He suggested this because where they were, there were so many coming and going, they didn't even have a chance to eat. So they boarded the ship and sailed over the Sea of Galilee to an area just outside of the city of Bethsaida. But the crowd saw them leave, and followed. They had seen so many miracles and healings that they wanted to stay near Him.

They ran on foot around the head of the lake and were so desperate, that some actually got to where Jesus was going before the boat carrying Him and the other men arrived. So when He came out of the boat and saw those who were already there, He was moved with compassion, because they were like sheep that didn't have a shepherd. So He began to teach them many things and heal their sick as well. As the day went on, the group grew larger until there were over 5,000 men, and thousands of women and children besides.

As the afternoon grew later and sunset approached, the Twelve came to Jesus, and said, "Dismiss the people because it's getting late and this is a deserted place. They can go to the nearby towns and villages to find places to stay and buy food and supplies, because they'll be hungry."

Then Jesus said, "They don't need to leave. You go ahead and give them something to eat."

Looking at the great crowd, He said to Philip, "Where can we buy bread so that these people can get something to eat?"

He said this to test him, because He knew what He was going to do.

The Apostle replied, "200 denarii, which would take ten months to earn, wouldn't be enough; and even then they would only get a little."

Jesus then asked, "How many loaves of bread do you actually have with you? Go and find out."

The Apostles came back with the answer.

"The only food we found was five barley loaves, and two small fish belonging to a little lad. But what good is that when we have so many to feed?"

The Lord said, "Bring them to me, and have the people sit down in groups of fifties and hundreds in open squares."

The multitude sat down in the grassy meadow as Jesus had instructed. Then He took the five loaves and two fish, looked up to Heaven, and blessed the food. Then He began to break the loaves, and gave them to His Apostles, who distributed the food to the crowd. He did the same with the fish. He kept on breaking and distributing the provisions until everyone was full.

When everyone was done eating, Jesus instructed His Apostles, "Gather up the pieces that are left over so that nothing will be lost."

They went about gathering what was left, and ended up with 12 baskets full of left-overs. While all this was happening, something else began to take place. It began among a few, and gradually continued to build. Having seen this amazing miracle, the men began to say to each other, "This Man is the Coming One. He is the Messiah."

The Lord realized that there were some who were about to come and take Him by force, and make Him King. The first thing He did was to immediately order His Apostles to get into the ship, and go ahead of Him to the other side. After they left, Jesus Himself dismissed the crowds, and then ascended into a mountain alone to meet with His Father in prayer.

Jesus prayed until it was the early hours before daybreak. As He stood to His feet, He gazed out onto the moonlit sea, where He could see His Apostles struggling. He had ordered them hours ago to depart for the other side, but they had run into a strong wind that was against them. They had made it halfway across the six mile trek, but could go no further.

A solitary figure descended from the mountain, approached the Sea of Galilee, and walked out onto the water. As the men continued to try to row against the contrary wind, they caught sight of what appeared to be a person passing by the ship, walking on the water. They thought it was a spirit, and screamed in terror. They heard a familiar voice calling out to them, "Take courage; it's only Me; stop being afraid."

Peter answered, "Lord, if it's you, command me to come out to you on the waves."

He replied, "Come."

The Apostle made his way down out of the ship, and stepped out onto the water. He began to actually walk on the water, away from the boat, and out towards Jesus. But when he saw how boisterous the wind was, fear began to take hold of him, and he began to sink. He cried out aloud, "Lord, save me."

Immediately, Jesus stretched out His hand, seized him, and stood him back on the water. Then He asked, "O you of little faith. Why did you doubt and waver?"

Peter and Jesus walked back, and were received back into the ship. As He stepped into the boat, the wind ceased, and immediately they were at their planned destination. The ones who had remained on the vessel were amazed beyond belief, because they hadn't considered the miracle of the loaves, since their hearts were hardened. They fell on their knees and worshipped him, saying, "Truly you are the Son of God."

*   *   *

After that eventful night, and going over the Sea of Galilee, they came to the rich four mile long and two mile wide plain of Gennersaret. They cast anchor off shore, and when they came off the boat the people recognized Who it was. Immediately the men of that place sent word throughout the whole territory round about, and soon there were people running everywhere, bringing the sick on their pallets out to where He was. Every place He went, there were sick people laying in the streets begging that they might just touch the hem of His garment, and all who did were healed.

In the meanwhile, those of the five thousand who had been fed miraculously came back to the seaside, near where the wonder was performed the day before, and waited for Jesus to appear. They assumed that He would be there because they had seen the Apostles leave on the boat without Him, and knew there were no other boats available for Him to travel on. But neither He nor His Apostles came, and so they got into ships and sailed over to Capernaum, looking for Him. They finally found Him in the Synagogue that Sabbath Evening, where He had been asked to teach. When He had finished speaking, those present were given permission to ask questions.

"Rabbi, when did you come here?"

Jesus ignored their question, and instead said, "I assure you, you aren't seeking Me because you saw miracles, but because you ate the loaves and satisfied your stomachs. Stop laboring for the food which perishes, but work for the food which abides unto eternal life, which the Son of Man will give you; for He is the One God the Father sealed."

Then they asked, "What are we to do so that we might do the works of God?"

"This is the work of God, that you believe on Him Whom He sent."

"What sign are you going to perform so that we may see and believe you? Our fathers ate the manna in the desert; as it is written, 'He gave them bread from Heaven to eat'."

"I assure you, it was not Moses who gave you the bread from Heaven; but My Father gives you the true Bread out of Heaven. For the bread of God is He Who comes down out of Heaven, and gives life to the world."

"Lord, give us this bread forever."

"I alone am the Bead of life. He who comes to Me shall never be hungry, and he who places his trust in Me shall never thirst. But I said to you that you have seen Me, and yet do not believe.

All that the Father gives Me shall come to Me, and the one who comes to Me I will positively not cast out.

For I came down from Heaven, not to do My Own will, but the will of Him Who sent Me. And this is the will of Him Who sent Me, that of all that He has given Me I shouldn't lose anything, but shall raise it up on the last day. And this is the will of My Father, that everyone who sees the Son and believes on Him may have life eternal, and I will raise Him up at the last day."

The Jews then began to grumble and mutter concerning Him, because He said, 'I alone am the bread which came down from Heaven.'

They kept on saying to one another, "Isn't this Jesus, the son of Joseph, Whose father and mother we know? Then how does He say He came down from Heaven?"

Jesus answered, "Stop grumbling and murmuring with one

another. No one is able to come to Me, unless the Father Who sent Me draw him. And I will raise him up on the last day. It is written in the Prophets, 'And they shall be taught by God.' Everyone who has heard and learned from the Father comes to Me. Not that anyone has actually seen the Father, except He Who has come from the presence of God. He has seen the Father.

I assure you, he that believes on Me has everlasting life. I alone am the Bread of Life. Your fathers ate the manna in the wilderness, and they died. This is the Bread which comes down from Heaven, in order that a person may eat of it, and not die. I alone am the Living Bread that came down from Heaven. If anyone eats of this bread he shall live forever. And the bread which I shall give is My flesh, which is given for the life of the world."

The Jews who had been murmuring began to dispute with each other, saying, "How can this man give us His flesh to eat?"

Jesus said to them, "I assure you, unless you eat the flesh of the Son of Man, and drink His blood, you don't have life in yourself. He who eats My flesh and drinks My blood has eternal life, and I will raise him up on the last day. For My flesh is truly food, and my blood is truly drink. He who continually eats My flesh and drinks My blood, continues to abide in Me and I in him. Even as the living Father has sent Me, and I live because of the Father; so he who eats Me shall also live because of Me. This is the bread that came down from Heaven; not the kind that your fathers ate, and died. He who eats this Bread will live forever."

Many of the ones who had been learning from Him and following His teaching up to this point, when they heard all this, said, "This teaching is offensive. Who can listen to it?"

When Jesus knew in Himself that even His pupils were grumbling about this, He said, "Does this offend you? What if you were to see the Son of Man ascend up to where He was before? It is the Spirit Who makes alive. The flesh is of no use at all. The words that I have spoken to you are spirit, and they are life. But there are certain among you who don't believe. Because of this I have told you that no one is able to come to Me unless it were given to him from the Father."

As a result of this, many of His disciples not only left the synagogue that night, but also stopped walking with Him altogether.

Then Jesus said to the Twelve, "You aren't going away also, are you?"

Peter said, "Lord, to whom shall we go? You have the words of eternal life. And we still believe and are sure that you are the Christ, the Son of the Living God."

Jesus responded, "Haven't I chosen you twelve? And one of you is a devil."

No one knew that day that Judas, son of Simon Iscariot, who was actually one of the Twelve, was already moving in the direction of betraying Him.

CHAPTER 20

Around that time, certain of the Scribes and Pharisees from Jerusalem came to Jesus because they were upset that some of His disciples had been seen eating bread with defiled hands, because they had not properly washed their hands. The Pharisees, and all the Jews, would not eat unless they washed their hands in a ritualistic fashion, which included washing one arm and then the other from the wrist down, by making a fist with the other hand. They were careful to observe this faithfully, because it was a tradition passed down from the elders. When they came from the market place, they wouldn't eat unless they washed this way, and there were many other instructions handed down about the cleaning of cups, pots, copper vessels, and even tables.

The Pharisees and Scribes asked Him, "Why do your disciples sidestep the traditions that have been handed down by the elders for us to observe? They don't wash their hands the proper way before they eat."

Jesus answered, "And tell me why do you sidestep the commandments of God Himself, because of the traditions that have been handed down to you? For God commanded, 'Honor your father and your mother,' and also, 'He who calls down curses upon father or mother, let him be executed'. But you say that if a son has something that he might give to his parents to help them like he is supposed to do, all he has to say is 'Corban,' which supposedly makes it a gift to God and then he is freed from giving it. He hasn't honored his parents at all. So you take away the authority from the Word of God because of your traditions.

Isaiah prophesied well about you as the ultimate hypocrites. It is written, 'This people draw near to me with their mouth, and honor Me with their lips, but they hold their hearts far away from Me. Their worship of Me is useless, while all they teach are the commandments of men'. You have abandoned the commandments of God, but you are careful to keep things like the washing of pots and cups and other things like that."

Then Jesus called the crowd back to Him, and said, "Listen to me, all of you. Understand that it is not something that is going into someone's mouth that makes a man unclean, but what comes out of a man's mouth. This is what defiles him. If any man has ears to hear, let him hear."

When Jesus went into Peter's house away from the people, the Apostles came to Him, and said, "Do you realize that the Pharisees were offended by what you said?"

Jesus said, "Every plant which My Heavenly Father doesn't plant shall be pulled up by the roots. Let them alone, they are blind leaders of the blind. And if a blind person is leading another blind person, they both fall into a ditch."

Peter requested, "Would you please explain the parable to us."

Jesus answered, "Don't you understand, either? Don't you understand that whatever enters a man from the outside cannot defile him, because it doesn't enter the heart but only the stomach, and afterward is eliminated?

But that which comes out of a man is what defiles him, because it comes from the heart. Out of the heart constantly comes evil thoughts, fornication, thefts, murders, adulteries, false testimonies, slanders, covetousness, wickedness, deceit, lasciviousness, an eye looking to do evil, pride, and foolishness. All these things come from within a man, and they do defile him. But to eat without washing your hands a certain way will never defile a man."

*   *   *

Jesus left Capernaum, and went north to the border of Tyre and Sidon. He had quietly entered into a home, because He didn't want anyone to know that He was there- but He couldn't be hidden. A Syro-Phoenician woman, who was Greek, had heard that Jesus was nearby and went to find Him, to get help for her daughter who was badly demonized.

When she found Him, she came up behind Him and cried out, "Have mercy on me, O Lord, Son of David, because my daughter is badly demonized."

But Jesus didn't say a word to her but just kept walking. She kept following and crying out to Him, begging Him to cast the demon out of her little girl.

As this went on, the Apostles said, "Send her away, because she keeps on crying out after us."

Jesus turned to her, and said, "I was only sent to the lost sheep of the house of Israel."

She fell on her knees at His feet, and said, "Lord, help me."

He replied, "Let the children be fed first. It's not right to take the children's bread, and throw it to their little pet dogs."

She said, "That's true. Yet the little dogs under the table eat the crumbs the little children drop."

Jesus answered, "Woman, your faith is great. Let it be as you wish. Go, the demon has gone out of your daughter."

When she returned home, she found the little child lying quietly on her bed, and the demon gone.

*   *   *

They journeyed north out of Galilee into Phoenicia itself, and on to the city of Sidon. He then went east towards Mount Hermon, and through one of its passes into the country of Herod Philip. He finally arrived in Decapolis, on the southeastern shore of the Sea of Galilee. There He went up into a mountain where He sat down, and large crowds came to Him. They brought with them people who were lame, maimed, blind, and dumb, as well as others with different illnesses. They hastily flung them on the ground at His feet and He healed them. The crowd marveled when they saw the dumb speak, the maimed made whole, the lame walking around, and the blind seeing, and they glorified the God of Israel.

In the midst of all this, they brought to Him one who was deaf and had a speech impediment. He took him away from the multitude to a private place. There He thrust His finger into his ears, spit, and touched his tongue. Then He looked up to Heaven, sighed, and said to him, "'Ephphatha,' which in Hebrew means, 'Be opened.' "

Immediately his ears were opened so that he could hear, and he began to speak clearly. Jesus charged them not to tell anyone about this, but the more He commanded them to be quiet, the more they proclaimed it wherever they went.

And all who heard about it were completely astonished, and said, "He has done all things well. He makes the deaf hear, and the dumb speak."

*   *   *

As His ministry in Decapolis continued, huge crowds again gathered around Him. At one point when they had been with

Him for three days, He said to His Apostles, "My heart goes out to these people because they've been with Me for three days, and they don't have anything to eat. And I don't want to send them away hungry because they might faint on the way home, since some came from far away."

The Apostles said, "Where in this wilderness, of all places, can we find enough bread to feed these thousands of people?"

Jesus asked, "How many loaves of bread do you have?"

They said, "Seven, and a few little fish."

He commanded the people to sit down on the ground. Then He took the loaves and fish, gave thanks, broke them, and gave them to His Apostles, who then gave them to the crowd. They all ate till they were full, and when the Apostles collected the leftovers, they ended up with seven baskets full. Afterwards, when the crowds were dismissed, Jesus and His men went on board the boat, and sailed to the regions of Magadan.

CHAPTER 21

When Jesus and His Apostles reached Dalmanutha on the western side of the Sea of Galilee, not far from Tiberias, the Pharisees and Sadducees came to question Him. They put Him to the test by demanding Him to show them a sign from Heaven.

He sighed, and said, "When it's evening, you say, 'there will be fair weather, for the sky is red.' And in the morning, 'today it will be stormy, for the sky is red and is filling with clouds.' Oh! You hypocrites! You understand how to discern the face of the sky, but you can't recognize the signs of the times.

Do you know the reason you seek for a sign? Because a wicked and adulterous generation craves for a sign, and none will be given, except the sign of the Prophet Jonah."

Then He abruptly sent them on their way and returned to the boat with His Apostles, to sail to the other side. As they travelled across the water, the Twelve realized that they had completely forgotten to bring bread to eat, and so they searched the boat for some, and found only one loaf on board.

Jesus began to charge them, "Listen and pay attention. Be on guard for the yeast of the Pharisees and the Sadducees, as well as the yeast of Herod."

They discussed what Jesus might have meant by this, and concluded, "It's because we didn't take any bread with us."

When He realized this was what they thought, He said, "O you of little faith, why are you reasoning that I said this because you don't have any bread? Don't you understand? Are your hearts still calloused and hardened? You have eyes, but do you see? And you have ears, but do you hear? Don't you remember? When I broke the five loaves among the 5,000, how many baskets of leftovers did you collect?"

They answered, "Twelve."

"And when I broke the seven loaves among the 4,000, how many baskets of leftovers did you collect?"

The Apostles answered, "Seven."

He then said, "Then how come you don't understand that I'm not speaking to you about loaves of bread, but that you should be on guard against the yeast of the Pharisees, Sadducees, and the Yeast of Herod?"

Then they understood that He wasn't speaking about guarding themselves against actual bread, but against the teaching of the Pharisees, Sadducees, and Herod.

*　　　*　　　*

They came to Bethsaida, on the eastern side of the Sea of Galilee, not far from where He had fed the 5,000 men. There they brought to Him a blind man and begged Him to touch the afflicted man. He caught the blind man by the hand and led him out of the village. Once there, He spit on his eyes, put His hands on him, and asked, "Do you see anything?"

Looking up, the man replied, "I see men, but they look like trees walking."

After that, Jesus put His hands again on his eyes and told him to look harder. He found out that his eyesight was restored to what it had been, and even the farthest things were clearly seen. He then sent him off to return to his own home, and said, "Don't go into town, nor tell anyone from the town what happened to you."

*　　*　　*

They left Bethsaida, and headed straight northward toward the road leading to Merom. As they ascended from Genneseret, leaving the Sea of Galilee behind, hills rose all around them. They turned north of the Sea, and west toward Kadesh Naphtali. As they climbed the steep hill above the marshes of Merom, before them was a lush plain of almost two thousand acres. They walked through some olive groves, up a gentle slope, and finally reached Kadesh. They had walked almost ten miles when they finally reached the Roman road that would take them to their destination.

They continued on for two days till they finally reached Caesarea Philippi, over 1100 feet above sea level. The area was surrounded by fig and mulberry trees; vines, and reeds, and water seemed to be everywhere. On the western side of a steep mountain which looked like a wall, was an immense cavern with a river thundering out of it, which was the upper source of the Jordan River. About 1000 feet above the cavern was the fortress of Caesarea Philippi. As they continued their journey through the nearby towns, Jesus stopped to pray, with His Apostles nearby. When He finished, he asked them, "Who do the people say that I, the Son of Man, am?"

They volunteered, "Some say John the Baptist, some, Elijah, and others say Jeremiah or one of the early prophets who has risen from the dead."

Then He asked, "But who do you say that I am?"

Peter answered, "You are the Christ, the Messiah, and the

Son of the Living God."

Jesus said to him, "Simon, son of Jonas, you are blessed, because flesh and blood did not reveal this to you, but My Father Who is in Heaven. And I say to you, you are Peter, and upon this rock I will build My Church, and the gates of hell shall not prevail against it. And I will give you the keys of the Kingdom of Heaven; and whatever you forbid to be done on earth, shall be forbidden in Heaven; and whatever you permit to be done on earth, shall be permitted in Heaven."

Then He commanded them to not tell anyone that He was Christ and Messiah. He also began to forewarn them about what was coming. For the first time, Jesus began to show His disciples that it was necessary for Him to go to Jerusalem and suffer many things. He would be rejected by the elders, chief priests, and Scribes; be killed, and be raised up on the third day.

Peter took Jesus apart privately and rebuked Him, "May mercy be shown to you Lord, this shall never happen to you."

The Lord abruptly wheeled around, turning His back on Peter, and said to him, "Be gone behind me and out of My sight, satan. You're a stumbling block to Me because you don't have a mind for the things of God, but for the things of men."

Then He said to all His Apostles, as well as others who were with them, "If anyone wants to come after Me as a follower of Mine, let him forget about himself and his own interests, take up his cross daily, and follow Me. For whoever wants to save his life will lose it; but whoever chooses to lose his life, for My sake and the Gospel, will find it.

For how does a man profit if he gains the whole world but loses his soul in the process? Or what shall a man give in exchange for his soul? For the Son of Man shall come in the glory of His Father with His angels, and then He will reward each and every man according to their works. For whoever is ashamed of Me and My words in this wicked and adulterous generation, the Son of Man shall also be ashamed of him, when

He comes in the glory of His Father with the holy angels.

But I tell you the truth, there are certain ones standing here right now, who will not die until they see the Son of Man come in His Kingdom with Power."

*   *   *

About a week later, Peter, James, and his brother John were climbing up Mount Hermon, the tallest in Israel. Jesus had asked them to accompany Him on this trek up the mountain so that He could pray. It was late in the afternoon when they had begun their journey, and by the time they reached the summit it was already nightfall.

After taking time to pray, the three Apostles fell into a deep sleep, but Jesus continued on. As He did, His appearance changed. His face shone like the sun, and His clothes were glittering and as white as snow. He was joined by Moses and Elijah, who appeared in Heavenly glory as well. They spoke with Him for a time about the decease He was to accomplish in Jerusalem. As they were having the conversation, the Apostles awoke and were startled and afraid by what they observed before them.

Peter didn't know what to say so he blurted out, "Lord, it's a good thing we're here. If you want, we can make three booths out of branches and leaves, one for You, one for Moses, and one for Elijah."

As he had begun to make his suggestion, the two Old Testament heroes departed, and a bright cloud enveloped the top of the mountain and the Apostles became even more afraid as they entered it.

Suddenly a voice thundered out of the cloud, "This is My beloved Son, in Whom I'm well pleased. Hear Him."

When the men heard it, they abruptly fell on their faces in terror.

Then they felt a touch and heard Jesus say, "Don't be afraid, you can get up."

So they lifted their eyes, looked around, and didn't see anyone else with them but Jesus, Who looked like He normally did again.

*   *   *

The next day as they were coming down the mountain, Jesus commanded them not to describe anything they had seen on the mountaintop to anyone, not even the other Apostles, until the Son of Man had risen from the dead. As they continued their descent, the three discussed among themselves what he meant by, "rising from the dead."

As they continued walking they asked, "Why are the Scribes always saying that Elijah must come first before the Messiah comes?"

Jesus answered, "That's true. Elijah does come first to restore all things. And he did come but they didn't recognize him and did whatever they wanted to him. And just as it's written, in the same way the Son of Man will suffer at their hands."

Then the three Apostles understood that when Jesus talked about Elijah, He meant John the Baptist.

When they came to the bottom of the mountain where He had left the other nine Apostles, Jesus saw a great crowd surrounding them and they were being questioned by some of the Scribes. When the people turned and saw Jesus coming, they were amazed that He had arrived at just the right moment. They ran to welcome Him. He approached the Scribes and demanded, "What are you talking with them about?"

Suddenly a man from the crowd fell to his knees and said, "Lord, have mercy on my son, my only son. He has a demon that makes it impossible for him to speak, and is an epileptic in a horrible condition. Whenever the demon lays hold of him he screams, and it throws him into convulsions, and he foams at the mouth and grinds his teeth. When he is done with the boy, he just lays motionless. I came to your Apostles and asked them to cast out the demon so that he would be healed, but they couldn't."

Jesus answered, "O faithless, perverse generation, how long shall I be with you and put up with you? Bring him to me."

As the boy was brought, he saw the Lord and the demon threw him down in a terrible convulsion. He fell to the ground rolling around and foaming at the mouth.

Jesus asked the father, "How long has this been happening to him?"

He answered, "Since he was a little boy. And often the demon will even throw him into the fire and into the water to try to destroy him. If you are able to do anything, please have mercy upon us and help us."

Jesus said, "The real question is not if I'm able, but if you are able. All things are possible to the one who is able to believe."

Immediately the boy's father cried out tearfully, "I believe, but please help my lack of faith."

When Jesus saw that the crowd had heard the man's cry and was running towards them to see what was happening, He rebuked the demon and said, "You dumb and deaf spirit, I order you to come out of him and never enter him again."

The demon cried out and threw him into severe convulsions and came out of him. The boy lay on the ground so still that many were saying that he was dead. But Jesus took him by the hand, lifted him, and he stood up; and He gave him back to his father. All those who stood watching were almost beside themselves with astonishment at the majesty of God that had been shown.

Later, after the crowd left and they had gone into the house, the Apostles came privately to Jesus and asked, "We have cast out demons before. Why couldn't we cast out this one?"

The Lord explained, "Because of your lack of faith. I assure you, if you have faith the size of a grain of a mustard seed, you will be able to say to this Mount Hermon, 'move from here to that other place over there,' and it will go. Not even one thing will be impossible to you. But this kind of demon only comes out by prayer and fasting."

CHAPTER 22

Again, they passed through Galilee on their way back to Capernaum, but Jesus didn't want anyone to be aware of it. His main concern was to teach His disciples.

He said to them, "Let these words sink down into your ears. The Son of Man is going to be betrayed into the hands of men. They will kill Him and after three days, He will rise."

They were extremely sorry each time they heard this. They really didn't understand it because the meaning of it was concealed from them, and they were afraid to ask Him to explain what he meant.

*   *   *

After returning to Capernaum, the ones who collected the Temple tax came to Peter and asked, "Doesn't your Teacher pay the Temple tax?"

Even though it was voluntary, every Jewish male who was

twenty years old and over was expected to pay the half-shekel tax to help maintain the Temple.

Peter responded, "Yes."

He then went home to talk with Jesus about it, but before he could say a word, Jesus said, "Simon, what do you think? Who do the kings of the earth collect taxes from, their children, or their subjects?"

Peter said, "From their subjects."

Jesus said, "So the children are supposed to be tax exempt, but we don't want people to get offended and think that we don't care about the Temple. Go down to the sea and throw in a hook, grab the first fish that comes up, and when you open its mouth, you'll find a shekel. Take that and pay the tax for the two of us."

When Jesus and the twelve came back to Peter's house, some of them came to Him and asked, "Who is the greatest in the Kingdom of Heaven?"

Jesus said, "Is that what you were arguing about on the road?"

They didn't say a word, because that was exactly what had been going on. Jesus knew what they were thinking about, and so He sat down and called all of the Apostles together. When they gathered around, Jesus called a child to come to Him and took him up into His arms.

"I assure you, unless you change your thinking and become as little children, you can't even enter the Kingdom of Heaven. So, whoever will humble himself like this little child, that is the person who is greatest in the Kingdom of Heaven. Whoever shall receive one of these little children in My Name, receives Me, and whoever receives Me also receives Him who sent Me."

John said, "Master, we saw a certain man casting out demons in Your Name and told him to stop because he's not one of us."

But Jesus said, "Stop hindering him. There is no man who will perform a miracle in My Name who will soon speak evil of Me, for he who is not against us is for us. Whoever will give you a cup of cold water to drink in My Name, because you belong to Christ, shall positively not lose his reward. But, on the other hand, whoever causes one of these little ones who believe in Me to stumble, it would be better for him to have a millstone hung about his neck, and that he would be drowned in the depth of the sea.

Woe unto the world because of stumbling blocks, for it is inevitable that stumbling blocks come, but woe to the man through whom the stumbling block comes. If your hand causes you to stumble, cut it off immediately. It is better for you to enter into life maimed, instead of having two hands and end up in the unquenchable fire of hell, where their worm doesn't die. And if your foot causes you to stumble, cut it off immediately. It's better for you to enter into life maimed, rather than having two feet to be thrown into hell, where the fire isn't quenched and their worm does not die.

And if your eye causes you to stumble, pluck it out and throw it from you. It is better for you to enter into life in the Kingdom of God with one eye, than to be cast into hell with two eyes, where the fire is not quenched and their worm does not die. Everyone will be salted with fire, and every sacrifice shall be salted with salt. Salt is good. But if the salt becomes saltless, what will you use to restore the saltiness to it? Have salt in yourselves, and be at peace with one another.

Be careful not to underestimate the value of one of these little ones, for I say to you, their angels always behold the face of My Father in Heaven. For the Son of Man has come to save that which was lost. What do you think? If a man owns one hundred sheep and one of them should wander off, wouldn't he leave the ninety-nine and go into the mountains looking for the one who went astray. And if he should find it, he rejoices more over that sheep than over the ninety- nine that didn't go astray. In the same way, it is not the will of your Father Who is in Heaven that one of these little ones should perish.

Furthermore, if your brother should commit a sin against

you, don't wait for him to come to you, but instead go to him, and show him his sin. Hopefully he will be convicted and confess it with just the two of you knowing about it, and you will have won your brother over. But if he will not hear you, take one or two others with you, so that in the mouth of two or three witnesses every word may be established. And if he is unwilling to hear them, tell the Church, and let him be to you as if he were a pagan and tax collector.

I assure you, whatever you forbid on earth shall likewise be forbidden in Heaven. And whatever you permit on earth shall also be permitted in Heaven. Again, I assure you, that if two of you on earth agree concerning anything they ask for, it shall be done for them from My Father in Heaven. For where two or three are gathered together in My Name, I am there in the midst of them."

*   *   *

Later that day, Peter came to Jesus and asked, "Lord, how often shall my brother sin against me and I forgive him? Would it be up till seven times?"

Jesus said to him, "I don't say to you, just up to seven times, but up to seventy times seven. Forgiveness in the Kingdom of Heaven is like a king who wanted to settle accounts with his slaves. And when he began to reckon with his accounts, one was brought to him who owed him millions of dollars. But since he didn't have enough to take care of it, his master commanded that the man be sold, along with his wife, children, and whatever he had, so that the debt could be paid. The servant fell on his knees and showed reverence to him and said, 'Lord, be patient with me, and I will pay you back all that I owe you.' Then the Lord of that servant was moved with compassion, released him, and completely cancelled the debt so that he didn't even have to repay it.

But that same servant went out and happened to meet one of

his fellow slaves who owed him a few dollars. He seized him, grabbed him by the throat, and started strangling him, saying, 'Pay me what you owe me,' but he couldn't, and he fell down at his feet and begged him, 'Be patient with me, and I will pay back all that I owe you.'

But he wasn't willing to do that, and instead threw him into prison till he paid the debt. When the other slaves saw what had happened, they were very sorry, and went to explain to their master all that had taken place.

Then his master called him in and said, 'You wicked servant, I cancelled your entire debt because you begged me to. Because of that, shouldn't you have shown mercy to your fellow slave, just as I was merciful to you?'

This made his master so angry that he handed him over to the torturers until he paid back all that he owed. That is what My Heavenly Father will do to you if you don't forgive every one of your brothers from your hearts."

CHAPTER 23

As the ministry of Jesus continued, He was journeying up a road when a disciple who was a Scribe approached, and said, "Master, I will follow you as a disciple wherever you go."

Jesus said to him, "Foxes have burrows, and the birds of the air have nests, but the Son of Man doesn't have a place to lay His head."

The Lord said to another of His disciples, "Follow Me."

But the man replied, "Lord, let me go and bury my father first."

Jesus said, "Let those who are dead bury their own dead, but you go everywhere and preach the Gospel of the Kingdom of God."

Another told Jesus, "Lord, I will follow with you as your disciple, but first let me go and say goodbye to those at home."

Jesus said, "No one who has put his hand on the plow and looks back to the things he left behind, is fit for the Kingdom of God."

*　　*　　*

The Jewish Feast of Tabernacles was approaching. His brothers, who didn't believe that He was the Messiah, said to Him, "You should leave Galilee and go into Judea, so that your disciples there might get the chance to see what you're doing. No man does things secretly if He is seeking to be known. In fact, since you are doing these works, make yourself known to the whole world."

He said to them, "My time isn't here yet, but it's always a good time for you. The world can't possibly hate you, but it does hate Me, because I'm the One testifying that its works are evil. You go up to the feast. As for Me, I'm not going yet, because My time hasn't fully come."

*　　*　　*

Jesus remained in Galilee for a few more days. When He did leave, He decided to travel privately. Instead of going through Perea to Jerusalem as most of the pilgrims would, He took the more direct route through Samaria. As He and His Apostles approached the first Samaritan village, He sent messengers on ahead to make sure everything was ready. The messengers returned to let Jesus know that He was not welcome, since He was on His way to Jerusalem.

When His Apostles James and John saw this, they said, "Lord, Do you want us to command fire to come down from Heaven, and consume them, like Elijah did?"

Jesus turned around and said to them, "You don't know what kind of spirit you are showing. For the Son of Man didn't come to destroy men's lives, but to save them." So they went on to another village.

*　　*　　*

In the meanwhile it was noticed that Jesus had not come with the caravan from Galilee. The Jews continued to seek Him though, saying, "Where is the One we have been hearing about?"

There was a great deal of murmuring among the crowds.

Some said, "He is a good man."

Others said, "No, He's not. He's leading the people astray."

But no one was talking openly about Him, because they were afraid of what the Jews might do to them. When the Feast had reached the midway point, Jesus arrived and went up to the Temple and began to teach.

The Jews marveled, saying, "How is it possible that this man knows these things without any formal education?"

He answered, "My doctrine doesn't come from Me, but belongs to the One Who sent Me. If any man wants to do His will, he shall know if the teaching is from God, or whether I am speaking from Myself. The one who is speaking from himself seeks his own glory. But He Who is seeking the glory of the One Who sent Him is the One Who is true, and no unrighteousness is in Him. Didn't Moses give you the Law? And yet not one of you is keeping it. Why are you trying to kill Me?"

The crowd replied, "You have a demon. Who's trying to kill you?"

Jesus answered, "I did one work, and all of you are marveling. Moses gave you circumcision, although he was only giving what the fathers had given; and even though it is the Sabbath, you will circumcise a man. Since a man can be circumcised on a Sabbath, so that the Law of Moses won't be broken, are you angry with Me, because I made a man completely whole on the Sabbath Day? Stop judging according to outward appearances, but judge with a righteous judgment."

Certain ones who lived in Jerusalem said, "Isn't this the One Who they are seeking to kill? And, look. He is speaking boldly, and they're not saying anything to Him. Surely the rulers haven't come to know that this man is truly the Messiah? But we know where this man is from. But when the Messiah comes, no one will know where He is from."

Jesus cried out with a loud voice, "You know Me, and where I am from; and I have not come by My own choice. But the One Who is true is the One Who sent Me, and Him you don't know. But I know Him because I am from Him, and He is the One Who sent Me."

Some of them wanted to take Him, but no one laid a hand upon Him because the hour had not come.

But many of the crowd believed on Him, and said, "When the Messiah comes, will He do more miracles than this Man has done?"

The Pharisees heard the crowd murmuring these things to each other about Him, and so they and the Chief Priests sent officers to take Him.

Jesus continued, "Yet a little while I am with you, and then I return to Him Who sent Me. You will seek Me and shall not find Me, and where I am you cannot come."

The Jews said among themselves, "Where does this man intend to go that we shall not find Him? He's not going to the Jews dispersed among the Gentiles or even to the Gentiles themselves, is He? And what does He mean by saying, 'You shall seek Me and you shall not find me', and 'Where I am, you cannot come'?"

*   *   *

The last day of the Feast of Tabernacles, the great day, had arrived. As daybreak came, the people in their festive clothes left the booths they had stayed in all week. God had commanded the Israelites to live in these shelters during this special week to remind them of how their ancestors lived while they were in the wilderness. Each had a citrus fruit in their left hand and a LULAB in their right, which was a cluster of myrtle, palm, and willow branches.

At the Temple, the pieces of the morning sacrifice were being laid out. At that moment, just as on each of the other days of the week long feast, there were three blasts of a trumpet heard, and a priest entered through the Water Gate carrying a golden pitcher he had filled with water from the Pool of Siloam. He proceeded into the Court of the Priests, where he was joined by another priest who carried the wine for the drink offering.

They both climbed to the altar and approached the silver funnels which led to the base of the altar. The wine was poured into the east funnel, and as the people shouted to the priest to raise his hand and pour the water, it was emptied into the west funnel. The people then joined the Levites in the "Great Hallel," which consisted of Psalm 113 to 118.

There was another three fold blast on the trumpet, and the people bowed down in worship. The priests circled the altar seven times, chanting, "O then, work now salvation, Jehovah! O Jehovah, send now prosperity!"

The people stood up, gave their own words of thanks and began to shake the LULAB towards the altar, causing the willow leaves to fall to the ground and the palm branches to break in pieces. Then a moment of silence followed, and a voice was heard that sounded through the Temple- the voice of the Rabbi from Nazareth.

"If anyone is thirsty, let him come to Me and drink. He who believes on Me, just as the Scriptures say, 'Out of his inmost being shall flow rivers of living water.'"

When they heard these words, many in the crowd said, "This man is truly the Prophet promised by Moses."

Others said, "This Man is the Messiah."

Still others said, "That can't be. The Messiah doesn't come from Galilee, does He? Doesn't the Scripture say that out of the family of David from Bethlehem, the city of David, the Messiah would come?"

While the people argued, the officers who had been sent to

take Jesus witnessed all this and left without Him. When they returned to the Chief Priests and Pharisees, the religious leaders asked, "Well, where is He? Why didn't you bring Him?"

The officers stated, "No man ever spoke like this Man speaks."

The Pharisees exclaimed, "Has He also deceived you? None of the rulers or the Pharisees have believed on Him, have they? But this crowd that doesn't know the Law is cursed."

Nicodemus, who was a ruler and a Pharisee, who was the one who had gone to speak to Jesus at night, spoke up. "Our Law doesn't pass judgment on a man until it hears from Him first, and knows what He is doing."

The other leaders retorted, "Are you from Galilee, too? Search the Scriptures for yourself, and see that no prophet arises out of Galilee."

At this they all left and went to their homes, while Jesus made His way towards the Mount of Olives.

CHAPTER 24

It was daybreak the next day when Jesus again entered the Temple. He sat down in the Court of the Women, near the Treasury, and a steady stream of people gathered. As He taught, the Scribes and Pharisees interrupted Him by bringing a woman who they had caught in the act of adultery, and standing her in the midst of the crowd for all to see.

"Teacher, this woman was caught in the very act of adultery. The Law of Moses says she should be stoned to death. What do you say?"

They were attempting to trick Him, so that they might accuse Him of wrongdoing. If He said she should be forgiven, they could say that He said it was all right to break the Law of Moses. If He said that she should be stoned to death, that would show He wasn't the teacher of love and mercy everyone thought He was. They felt that He had no way out of this dilemma.

At first Jesus didn't say a word. He just stooped down, bent forward with His head down, and wrote on the ground. They asked again what should be done to the sinful woman. Finally Jesus said, "She should be stoned to death."

As the religious leaders began to feel the pleasure of finally succeeding in trapping Him, He added, "The one of you who has never sinned should throw the first stone."

He then resumed his writing on the ground, with His head bowed down. When the religious leaders heard this, they were convicted by their own conscience. One by one they began to walk away, beginning from the oldest, until the only ones left were Jesus and the accused woman.

When Jesus finally looked up and saw that the only one left was the woman, He asked, "Woman, where are the ones who accused you? Didn't anyone condemn you?"

She said, "No one, Lord."

He said, "I don't condemn you either. Go your way, and don't sin anymore."

*　　　*　　　*

Later in the day, Jesus was once again teaching. But this time He was occupying one of the Temple porches.

"I alone am the light of the world. He who makes a habit of following Me shall not walk in darkness, and shall not only see the light of life, but shall possess it."

The Pharisees said, "You bear testimony of yourself, so your testimony isn't true."

Jesus replied, "Even if I bear testimony of Myself, My testimony is true: because I know where I came from, and where I'm going. But you don't know where I came from, nor where I'm going. You make a habit of judging according to the flesh. I judge no one. But even if I do pass judgment, My judgment is true, because I am not alone, but I have Him Who sent Me. And in your own Law it's written, that the testimony of two men is true. I am one Who bears witness of Myself, and the

Father Who sent Me bears witness of Me, as well."

"Where is your Father?"

"You don't know me, nor My Father; but if you had known Me, you would have known My Father also."

Jesus spoke these words in the Treasury where He could have easily been arrested, but no one laid a hand on Him because His hour hadn't come yet.

He continued, "I will leave, and you will seek Me, and you'll die in your sins. Where I'm going, you can't come."

The Jews said, "How can He say we're not able to go where He is going, unless He's planning on killing Himself."

"You are from beneath, and I am from above. You are of this world, but I'm not. Therefore I said to you, you shall die in your sins: for if you don't believe that I am He, you shall die in your sins."

"Who are You?"

"I am what I said from the beginning. I have many things to say and to judge concerning you. But He Who sent Me is true, and I speak to the world the things I hear directly from Him."

As He spoke these things, many believed what He said. Then Jesus said to the Jews that believed what He said, "If you continue in My Word, then you are truly My disciples. And you shall know the truth, and the truth shall make you free."

They answered, "We are Abraham's offspring, and have never been in bondage to anyone. How is it that you say, 'you shall be made free.'?"

"I assure you, everyone who makes a habit of sinning is a slave of sin. And the slave does not have a permanent place in the house: but the son abides forever. Therefore if the Son makes you free, you will be really free.

I know that you are Abraham's offspring, but you are trying to kill Me, because My word has no place in you. I speak about what I have seen with My Father, and you do the things which you have heard from your father."

"Our father is Abraham."

"If you really were the children of Abraham, you would do what Abraham would do. But you want to kill Me, a man who has told you the truth which I heard from God. Abraham would not do things like that. You do the deeds of your father."

"We were not born out of fornication. We have one Father – God Himself."

"If God were your Father, then you would love Me: because I came from God. I didn't make the decision to come, He did and, so, here I am. Why don't you understand the way I speak? Because you're not able to hear My Word.

You are of your father the devil, and you want to do what he wants. He was a murderer from the beginning, and does not stand in the truth, because there is no truth in him. When he tells a lie, he is speaking from his own possessions: because he is not only a liar, but the father of all lies. And because I tell you the truth, you don't believe Me. Which of you convicts Me of sin? And if I say the truth, why don't you believe Me? The one who is of God hears God's Words: and this is why you don't hear them, because you are not of God."

Then the Jews said, "Aren't we saying it beautifully when we say you're a Samaritan, and have a demon?"

"I don't have a demon; but I honor My Father, and you are dishonoring Me. I am not seeking My Own glory. There is One Who seeks and judges. I assure you, if anyone keeps My Word, he shall positively never see death."

"Now we definitely know that you have a demon. Abraham died, and so did the prophets. But you say, if a person keeps My Word, he shall positively never taste death. You're not greater than our father Abraham who died, are you? And the prophets died also. Who do you make yourself out to be?"

"If I honor Myself, My honor is nothing. It is My Father Who honors Me; of whom you say, 'He is our God.' You have not known Him before, and you still don't know Him. Suppose I say that I don't know Him; I would be a liar like you. But I do know Him, and keep His Word. Abraham, your Father, rejoiced to see

My day; and he saw it, and was glad."

"You're not fifty years old yet, and you've seen Abraham?"

Jesus stated, "I assure you, before Abraham was born, I Am."

They ran from the Porch into the Court of the Gentiles to get stones to throw at Him, but Jesus hid Himself and made His way out of the Temple.

CHAPTER 25

The next day was the Sabbath, and Jesus and His Apostles ascended the Temple Mount. As they came near to the building, Jesus noticed a man who had been blind since birth. Normally the man would have been begging for alms, but today he sat in silence because it was the Sabbath.

The Apostles asked Him, "Master, was it this man, or his parents who sinned, that caused him to be born blind?"

Jesus replied, "This man didn't sin, and neither did his parents. He was born this way so that the works of God might be openly shown in him. It's necessary for us to be doing the works of Him Who sent Me, while it is still day. The night comes, when no one is able to work. As long as I am in the world, I am light to the world."

After He said, this He spat on the ground and used the saliva to make clay. Then He walked over to the man and spread the clay on his eyes, and told the man, "Go and wash your eyes in the Pool of Siloam."

So he made his way to the southern end of Jerusalem, where the Pool was located. At 53 feet long, 18 feet wide, and 20 feet deep, it was the smallest of all the pools in the city. When he arrived, he washed the mud from his eyes, and could then see. When he returned to where he had met Jesus, he was seen by his neighbors and some others who knew that he had been blind.

They said, "Isn't this the blind man who always sat here and begged?"

Some said, "Yes, that's him."

Others said, "That's impossible. It's just someone who looks like him."

But then the man spoke up for himself, "That was me."

They asked, "How were your eyes opened?"

He answered, "A man called Jesus made clay, spread it on my eyes, and said to me, 'Go to Siloam and wash.' So I went, washed as He told me to, and now I received my sight."

"Where is He?"

"I don't know."

They brought the one who had once been blind to the Pharisees. It had been the Sabbath when Jesus made the clay and opened his eyes. The Pharisees also asked him about how he received his sight.

He explained, "He placed clay on my eyes, I washed, and now I can see."

Some of the Pharisees said, "This man is not from God, because He doesn't keep the Sabbath."

Others said, "How can a man who is a sinner perform such miracles?"

As the argument continued, they asked the blind man, "Since it was your eyes that He opened, what do you have to say about Him?"

He answered, "He is a prophet."

Now the Jews didn't believe that he had actually been blind, and received his sight.

So they called his parents and asked, "Is this man your son, who they say was born blind? How can he see now?"

The parents were afraid of the Jews, because the Jews had agreed to have anyone who confessed that Jesus was Messiah to be put out of the synagogue. So they said, "We are sure that this is our son. And we know for a fact that he was born blind. But how he can now see, and who gave him his sight, we don't know. Ask him. He is old enough to speak for himself."

So they called the man who had been healed back in a second time, and said, "Give glory to God, because we are positive that this man is a sinner."

"Whether He is a sinner or not, I don't know. But there is one thing I do know. I used to be blind, and now I can see."

"What did He do to you? How did He open your eyes?"

"I already told you and you didn't hear. Why do you want to hear it again? Do you also want to be His disciples?"

"You may be a disciple of His, but we are Moses' disciples. We are positive that God spoke to Moses, but we don't even know where this man came from."

"That's amazing. He opened my eyes, and you don't know where He's from. We know absolutely that God doesn't hear sinners, but if someone is a worshipper of God and makes a habit of doing His will, God will hear him. Since the world began, has anyone ever heard of a person who was born blind, having their eyes opened? If this man was not from God, He wouldn't be able to do anything."

"You who were completely born in sin, are you trying to teach us?"

They threw the man out of the meeting. When Jesus heard what happened, He went looking for him. When he found him, He asked, "Do you believe on the Son of Man?"

"Who is He, Sir, that I may believe in Him."

"You have seen Him, and in fact He is the One speaking to you right now."

He said, "Lord, I believe," fell down, and worshipped Him.

"I came into this world for judgment, in order that those who can't see, might see; and those who can see, might be blinded."

Some of the Pharisees who were there with Jesus overheard what He had said, and replied, "We're not blind, are we?"

Jesus said, "If you were blind, you would have no sin. But since you say you can see, your sin remains. I assure you, he who does not enter by the door into the sheepfold, but climbs up from some other way, that one is a thief and a robber. But he who enters through the door is the shepherd of the sheep. The doorkeeper opens to this one. And the sheep hear His voice, and He calls His sheep by name, and leads them out. Whenever he lays hold on His own sheep and puts them forth, He goes before them, and the sheep follow Him, because they know His voice. They will not follow a stranger, but will run from him, because they don't know his voice."

Since those listening didn't understand the meaning of the parable He was giving them, Jesus said, "I assure you, I alone am the Door to the sheep. All that came before Me are thieves and robbers, but the sheep didn't listen to them. I alone am the Door. If anyone enters by Me he shall be saved, and shall go in and out, and shall find food. The thief comes only to steal, kill, and destroy; but I alone came that they might have life in superabundance. I alone am the Good Shepherd. The Good Shepherd lays down His life for the sheep. But the one who is a paid helper, and not the shepherd, doesn't own the sheep. So when he sees a wolf approaching, he leaves the sheep and runs, because he is only a paid helper, and doesn't care for the sheep. The wolf snatches them up and scatters them.

I alone am the Good Shepherd, and I know the sheep that are mine, and they know Me. As the Father knows Me, even so I know the Father. I lay down My life for the sheep. There are other sheep that I have which are not of this sheepfold. It's necessary for Me to lead them, and they will listen to My voice. They will come to be only one flock with only one Shepherd. On account of this My Father loves Me, because I lay down My life in order that I might take it again. No one takes it from Me, but I lay it down Myself. I have authority to lay it down, and authority to take it again. This commandment I received from My Father."

CHAPTER 26

As He prepared to leave Jerusalem and journey into other parts of Judea, Jesus appointed 70 others aside from the Twelve, and sent them two by two before His face into every city and place He was planning to go.

He said to them, "The harvest truly is great, but the laborers are few. So pray to the Lord of the Harvest that He will thrust out workers into His harvest. Be on your way. Look, I am sending you out as lambs in the middle of wolves. Don't carry a purse, nor a begging bag, nor a change of sandals: and don't get involved in long, drawn-out greetings.

In whatever home you enter, first say, 'Peace be to this home.' If the head of the household is a person of peace, your peace shall rest upon him; but if he's not, it shall return to you. Don't make a habit of changing from one home to another. In that same house remain a guest, eating and drinking what is set before you, for the workman is worthy of his pay. In whatever city you enter, and they welcome you, eat what is set before you: and heal those that are ill, and say to them, 'The Kingdom of God has come near.'

But into whatever city you go, and they don't welcome you, go out into the main streets, and say, 'Even the very dust of your city, which clings to our feet, we wipe off against you. Nevertheless, be sure of this, the Kingdom of God has come near.' I say to you, it will be more endurable in that day for Sodom, than for that city.

Woe to you, Chorazin; woe to you, Bethsaida; because if the miracles that were done in you had been done in Tyre and Sidon, they would have repented in sackcloth and ashes long ago. But it will be more endurable for Tyre and Sidon on the Day of Judgment, than for you. And as for you, Capernaum, will you be exalted to Heaven? No, you shall be thrust down to the depths of misery and disgrace in hell.

Anyone that hears you hears Me. And all who reject you reject Me: and he who rejects Me rejects the One Who sent Me."

*   *   *

Some days later Jesus met up with the 70, who had returned overflowing with joy. They exclaimed, "Lord, even the demons obey our orders in Your Name."

Jesus said to them, "I observed satan fall from Heaven like lightning. Behold, I have given you authority to walk on snakes and scorpions, and over all the power of the enemy. Nothing, and I mean nothing, will in any case harm you. Nevertheless, don't rejoice because the demons obey your orders, but rejoice that your names are written down in Heaven."

At that very hour, Jesus was filled with the joy of the Holy Spirit, and said, "I thank and praise you, Father, Lord of Heaven and Earth, because you hid these things from the wise and educated, and revealed them to the untaught. Yes, Father, You wanted it to be so, because it was your good pleasure. All things were delivered to Me by My Father: and no one knows Who the Son is, except the Father; and Who the Father is, except the Son, and whoever the Son desires to reveal Him to."

Then He turned to the Twelve and said to them, privately, "Blessed are the eyes which see the things you're seeing, for I say to you, many prophets and kings desired to see the things which you see, and didn't see them; and to hear the things which you hear, and didn't hear them."

At that, behold, a certain teacher of the Mosaic Law stood to his feet and put Jesus to the test by asking, "Teacher, what do I have to do to inherit eternal life?"

Jesus said, "What is written in the Law? How do you interpret it?"

"You shall love the Lord your God with your whole heart, your whole soul, all your strength, and your whole mind; and your neighbor as yourself."

"Correct. Make a habit of doing this and you'll live."

But the lawyer desired to show that he was righteous to those listening, and so he said, "And who is my neighbor?"

Jesus answered, "A certain man went down from Jerusalem to Jericho. As he continued on mile after mile descending down into the Jordan Valley, he suddenly found himself surrounded by robbers who attacked and wounded him. They stripped him of his clothes and took everything else he had, leaving him lying there half dead.

Now it just so happened, a certain priest was going down that road, and when he saw him, he stepped over to the other side of the road and passed on. And, likewise, a Levite came down to the place and came close enough to see the wounded man, and then he also crossed over to the opposite side of the road and continued on.

But a certain Samaritan, as he journeyed, came down to the place where the wounded man was, and when he saw him, was moved with compassion. He came to him, poured oil and wine on his wounds, and bound them up. He hoisted him up on his own beast of burden, and led him up the Jericho Road to an inn where he took care of him. On the next day, he took out two silver coins, gave them to the innkeeper, and said, 'Take care of him, and if you have to spend any more than this, don't trouble this man for the difference. I will repay you when I return this way.' Which of the three, do you think, proved to be a neighbor to the one attacked by the robbers?"

The lawyer replied, "The one who showed mercy to him."

Jesus said, "You go and do likewise."

*   *   *

Bethany was a suburb of Jerusalem, located only a few miles away from the Holy City. Jesus had received an invitation to stay at the home of a woman named Martha, who lived with her sister Mary and her brother Lazarus. He arrived, and a reception was held in His honor. As Jesus talked with the other guests, Martha scurried around, and seemed to be going around in circles serving people. While she was completely preoccupied with serving, her sister Mary sat at Jesus' feet, drinking in everything He said. It seemed to Martha that her younger sister was being irresponsible, and she grew more and more upset.

Finally the older woman burst in upon Jesus, stood before Him, and said, "Lord, doesn't it bother you that my sister has left me to do all the work? Tell her to get up and come help me."

Jesus answered sympathetically, "Martha, Martha, you're worried and distracted by so many things. But there is really only one thing that's necessary, and that's the part Mary has chosen, and it will not be snatched away from her."

*   *   *

As they journeyed, they came near Perea, where John the

Baptist had baptized so many, including Jesus Himself and some of His Apostles. As Jesus finished praying one day, one of His disciples approached.

"Lord, John taught his disciples how to pray. Will you teach us?"

He answered, "When you pray, say, 'Our Father, Who is in Heaven, may Your Name be kept sacred and honored. Cause your kingdom to come, and Your will to be done. Give us each day the bread we need, and forgive us our sins as we make a habit of forgiving those indebted to us. Don't lead us into temptation, but deliver us from evil'.

Which of you who has a friend shall go to him at midnight, and say, 'since you're my friend, would you please lend me three loaves of bread, because a friend of mine who's on a journey showed up at my door unexpectedly. The problem is that I don't have any food to offer him.' I say to you that even though he won't give you anything because he is your friend, he'll give you as many as you need because you won't stop asking.

I say to you, keep on asking and it shall be given. Keep on seeking and you will find. Keep on knocking and it shall be opened to you. For everyone who keeps on asking, receives; he who keeps on seeking, finds; and the one who keeps on knocking will have the door opened to him.

If a son asks any of you who is a father for a fish, he won't give him a snake instead, will he? Or if he asks for an egg, will he give him a scorpion? If you then who are evil know how to give good gifts to your children, how much more will your Father Who is in Heaven give the Holy Spirit to those that ask Him?"

*   *   *

On another day, He was brought a man who was unable to speak because of a demon he was possessed by. When the demon was cast out, the man began to speak, and the crowd marveled. Some said, "Beelzebub, the prince of the demons, gave Him the power to do this."

Others put Him to the test by demanding some spectacular miracle from Heaven. But He knew what they were thinking and why they were asking for this. So He said, "Every kingdom divided against itself is brought to ruin, and a house divided against itself falls. Now assuming that satan is divided against himself, which he must be if he is giving Me the power to cast out demons, how will his kingdom stand? And, again, assuming that I am casting out demons by the power of Beelzebub, by whose power do your sons cast them out? They'll be your judges. But if I cast out demons by the finger of God, then the kingdom of God has come upon you unexpectedly.

When the strong man, who is fully armed, guards his home, his possessions are safe. But when the stronger one comes upon him and overcomes him, he takes away all the armor he placed his confidence in, and then divides his goods with others. He who is not with Me is against Me and the one who doesn't gather with Me scatters.

When the unclean spirit has come out of a man, he goes through waterless places looking for rest, and when he doesn't find any, he says, 'I'll return to the house I came out of.' And when he comes, he finds it swept, cleaned, and in order. Then he goes, finds seven spirits more wicked than he is, and they all enter into him and settle down permanently. So the last state of that man becomes worse than it was at first."

As Jesus was speaking, a woman in the crowd raised her voice, and said, "Blessed is the womb that bore you, and the breasts from which you nursed."

But He said, "The ones who are really blessed are the ones who hear the Word of God and are careful not to break it."

*   *   *

While the people were gathering together in crowds that were getting larger and larger, Jesus began to speak to them, "This is an evil generation. They are constantly demanding a miracle, and no miracle will be given, except the miracle of the prophet Jonah. For just as he was a supernatural sign to the Ninevites, the Son of Man shall also be to this generation.

The Queen of the South shall rise up in the judgment with the men of this generation, and shall condemn them, because she came from the most remote parts of the earth to hear the Wisdom of Solomon; and, look, Someone greater than Solomon is here. The men of Nineveh shall rise up in the judgment with the men of this generation, and shall condemn them, because they repented at Jonah's preaching; and, look, someone greater than Jonah is here.

No one, after he lights a lamp, puts it in a cellar or under a grain measure, but on a lampstand, so that those who come in from time to time can see the light. The lamp of the body is the eye. When your eye has a single focus, your whole body is well lit. But when your eye is evil, your body is full of darkness. So be careful that the light that is in you is not actually darkness. If your body is well lit without a hint of darkness, the whole shall be full of light, like when a lamp is brightly shining and giving you light.

CHAPTER 27

As the morning prayers in the synagogue ended on that Sabbath, a Pharisee approached the Lord and invited Him to his home for breakfast. Jesus came in and sat down at the table, and his host was amazed that Jesus hadn't taken part in the ceremonial handwashing, which was traditional among the Jews.

Jesus said to him, "You Pharisees make a habit of cleaning the outside of the cup and plate, but your inward part is full of plunder and wickedness. You fools, didn't the One that made what was outside, also make the inside? Instead, give alms to the poor from what is inside the cup and plate, and, look, all things are then clean to you.

But woe to you, Pharisees, because you pay a tenth of mint and rue and every other kind of herb, but you neglect justice and the love of God. You ought to be tithing, but you shouldn't have left the other part undone. Woe to you, Pharisees, because you prize the most important seats in the synagogue reserved for the Teachers of Moses' Law, as well as respectful greetings in the market places that are given to those who are important. Woe to you, Scribes and Pharisees, hypocrites! You are like unseen tombs that ceremonially defile the men that walk over them, because they're not aware of them."

Then one of the experts in the Old Testament Law said, "Teacher, by saying these things you're insulting us, too."

He responded, "Woe to you also, you interpreters of Moses' Law, because you load men down with the burden of precepts that are hard to bear, and you wouldn't even touch one with one finger. Woe to you! Because you're building the sepulchers of the prophets, and it was your fathers that killed them. So you are witnesses and give full approval of what your fathers did: because they killed the prophets, and you build their memorials.

On account of this, God, in His wisdom, said, 'I will send them prophets and apostles. Some of them they will persecute and even kill; so that the blood of all the prophets, which has been shed since the foundation of world, may be required from this generation. Beginning with the blood of Abel to the blood of Zechariah, who perished between the altar of burnt offering and the Sanctuary: it shall all be required of this generation.' Woe to you, experts in the Law of Moses, because you have locked the door to the house of knowledge and taken away the key. By doing this, you don't go in, and you keep those who want to enter from going in."

After He said these things, the Scribes and Pharisees were enraged at Him and set themselves against Him. They began to provoke Him by asking Him question after question, not giving Him the chance to consider His answers, and trying to put words in His mouth. They were waiting for the chance to catch Him in something He said, so that they could accuse Him. In the meanwhile, thousands of people gathered to hear the exchange between Jesus and the religious leaders. There were so many present that they were trampling each other underfoot.

Jesus began to speak to the His disciples first of all: "Beware of the yeast of the Pharisees, which is hypocrisy; because there is not even one thing that seems to be covered up, which shall not be uncovered; nor hidden, that shall not be made known. All the things you have spoken in darkness shall be heard in the light. And that which you whispered in someone's ear in the secret place shall be shouted from the housetops.

But I say to you who are my friends, don't be afraid of the ones who can kill the body and then can't do anything else. But I will warn you about who you should fear. It's Him who after the killing has the authority to throw someone into hell. He is the One you should fear. Aren't five little sparrows sold for one cent, and every one of them is under the watchful care of God? In fact, even all the hairs of your head have been counted. Stop being afraid; you are much more important than many sparrows.

Also, I say to you, whoever shall declare openly and freely his oneness with Me before men, the Son of Man will openly and freely declare His oneness with him before the angels of God. But he that denies Me before Men shall be denied before the angels of God. And whoever speaks a word against the Son of Man can be forgiven, but whoever blasphemes the Holy Spirit shall not be forgiven. And when they bring you to the synagogues, and to the magistrates, and authorities, don't be worried about what you'll say to defend yourself. The Holy Spirit will teach you in that very hour what you ought to say."

Now a certain person in the crowd said to Christ, "Teacher, tell my brother to divide the inheritance with me."

He replied, "Man, who appointed Me a judge or arbiter over you?"

Then He said to the multitude, "Take heed, and guard yourself against greed: for a man's life doesn't consist in the abundance of the possessions he enjoys.

The land of a certain rich man was fertile and produced

bountiful crops. He thought over and over saying, 'what will I do, because I don't have enough room to store all my crops?' Finally he decided, 'I know what I'll do. I'll pull down my barns and build greater ones where I can store my grain and goods. Then I'll say to my soul, 'soul, you have many good things that will last many years. Take it easy. Eat, drink, and be merry.' But God said to him, 'you fool. This very night your soul will be demanded from you. Now who will get to own all these things you prepared and possessed?' This will be the case for anyone who hoards up treasure for himself, and is not rich with what God considers true riches."

Then He turned His attention to His disciples, and said, "On account of this, I say to you, stop worrying about your life: what you shall eat, or what will you put on your body. Life is more than food, and the body is more than clothing. Consider the ravens. They neither sow nor reap, nor have store houses nor barns. God feeds them; and how much more important are you than birds?"

Also, which of you is able to add to his height by worrying? If you're not able to do even what would be the least thing, why do you worry about all the rest? Consider the lilies; they neither spin nor weave, and yet I say to you that Solomon in all of his glory didn't clothe himself like one of these. So if God clothes the grass of the field, which exists today and tomorrow is thrown into the oven, how much more will He clothe you, the ones who have so little faith?

Now, you stop striving about, 'what will we eat?', and, 'what will we drink?'; and stop going back and forth from hope to fear, because all the nations of the world seek after these things. And, besides, your Father knows that you need these things. But instead seek for His kingdom, and all these things will be added to you. Sop being afraid, little flock, because your Father has chosen to give you the kingdom.

Sell what you have, and give alms. Provide for yourselves moneybags that don't wear out, a treasure in Heaven so it won't fail, where no thief can approach and steal it, and no moth destroys it. For where your treasure is, that's where your heart will be also. See to it that your clothes are fastened around you with a belt, and that your lamps are already lit and constantly burning.

Be like men waiting for their master, who has gone to a wedding feast: so that when he comes back and knocks, they will be ready to open it for Him immediately. Blessed are those servants, who will be alert and watching when their master returns. I assure you, He will fasten His garments about Himself with a belt, and will cause them to sit down at the table, and serve them food and drink. And if He shall come in the second or third watch of the night, when people are usually in their deepest sleep, and shall find them alert, He will bless them.

And know this, if the owner of a house knew what hour a thief was coming, he would never allow his house to be broken into. So you need to always be ready because the Son of Man is coming in an hour when you don't think He will."

Peter asked, "Lord, are you giving this parable only to us, or does it include everyone else as well?"

The Lord said, "Who then is a wise and trustworthy steward, whom His Lord will place over His household servants, to give them their food at the proper time? The servant who is found doing this very thing when his Master comes will be blessed. Truly I say to you, He will give him responsibility over all His possessions.

But if that servant says in his heart, 'my Master won't be coming back for a long time'; so he begins to beat the male and female slaves, and to eat, and drink, and get drunk; the Master of that servant will come in a day when he wasn't looking for Him, and will punish that servant, and give him his part with those who are untrustworthy.

Now that servant, which knew what his master wanted done, but didn't even prepare to do, much less actually do it, will be beaten with many stripes. But the one who didn't know what his Master wanted done, and did something that deserved punishment, will receive fewer stripes. Because to whom much is given, much will be required: and the one who was entrusted with much will be asked to give more.

I came to send fire on the earth, and how I wish that it was already burning. But I have a baptism to be baptized with, and I am hard pressed to see it accomplished. Do you think that I came to bring peace to the earth? Not at all: I tell you that I came to bring division. From this time on there will be five in a house divided, three against two, and two against three. The father shall be divided against a son, and son against a father; a mother against a daughter, and daughter against a mother; a mother in law against a daughter in law, and a daughter in law against her mother in law."

He spoke on to the crowd, "Whenever you see the cloud arising out of the west, you immediately say, 'a thunderstorm is coming', and that's what happens. And when a south wind begins to blow, you say, 'it's going to be hot', and so it is. You hypocrites, you can discern and interpret the face of the sky, but you can't read this significant time.

And why aren't you able to even judge what is right? While you're on your way to court with your opponent, try to be released from the lawsuit, lest at any time he drag you in front of the judge; because he may then hand you over to the officer, who is assigned to inflict punishment, and then throw you into prison. I tell you, you won't leave that place until you have paid the very last penny."

There were some present who told Jesus about some Galileans who were killed by Pontius Pilate while offering sacrifices in the Temple, so that it was said that their blood had been mingled with their sacrifices.

Jesus said, "Do you think that these Galileans were worse sinners than the rest of those in Galilee, because they suffered these things? Not at all. I tell you, you will all perish just like them, if you don't repent. What about the eighteen people who had the tower in Siloam fall on them? Do you think they were worse sinners than the rest of those living in Jerusalem? Not at all. Unless you repent, you will all perish like them."

Then He presented this parable: "A certain man had a fig tree planted in his vineyard; and he came looking for fruit on it, but didn't find any. He said to the vinedresser, 'Look, I have been seeking for fruit from this tree for three years, and haven't found any. Cut it down; because not only does it not produce fruit, but it keeps the other trees from producing more, by using nutrients they could use.' But the vinedresser answered, 'Lord, let it alone for one more year, and I'll dig around it, and throw in some manure. After that, if it produces fruit, good; but if not, then you can cut it out.'"

CHAPTER 28

Another Sabbath came, and Jesus stood in one of the local synagogues, teaching. Among those who were present was a woman who was completely bent over because of a curvature of her spine. She had been like this since the time a demon had caused it 18 years earlier, and it was impossible for her to raise herself up at all. When Jesus saw her, He called her to come to Him.

When she reached Him, He said, "Woman, you have been released permanently from your infirmity."

He placed His hands upon her, and immediately her crooked back was completely straightened. She began to glorify God for His wonderful blessing. But the ruler of the synagogue was outraged that Jesus had healed on the Sabbath Day, and said to the crowd, "There are six days when it's proper to get things done. During those days you should come and be healed, but not on the Sabbath Day."

Jesus answered, "You hypocrite, doesn't each one of you on

the Sabbath release his ox or donkey from the stall and lead it out to get a drink? This woman, who is a daughter of Abraham, has been bound by satan for, think of it, 18 long years. She simply had to be released, even though it was the Sabbath."

As He said these things, all those who had opposed Him were completely embarrassed and ashamed: and the rest of the crowd began to rejoice because of all the glorious things He was doing.

Then He said, "What is the Kingdom of God like? It is like a grain of mustard seed, which a man took, and threw into his garden. And it grew until it became as large as a great tree; and the birds of heaven made their nests in the branches. What shall I liken the Kingdom of God to? It is like the yeast, which a woman took and hid in three measures of wheat flour, until the whole thing was filled with yeast."

*   *   *

Jesus came to Jerusalem that winter for the Feast of Dedication, called Hanukkah. He was walking among the people on Solomon's Porch that Herod had added to the Temple complex, so that it could hold more people. As He walked around on the covered porch, He passed in front of the Beautiful Gate, the main entrance into the Court of the Women.

He suddenly found Himself surrounded by the Jews, who said, "How long are you going to hold us in suspense? If you are the Christ, then say so."

He replied, "I told you, and you didn't believe Me. The works that I'm doing in My Father's Name bear witness of Me. As I already told you, you don't believe because you are not of My sheep. My sheep make a habit of listening to My voice; I know them, and they follow Me on the same road that I take. I give them life that's eternal; and they shall never, ever perish; and it's impossible for anyone to snatch them out of My hand. My Father, Who gives them to Me as a gift, is greater than all; and it is impossible for anyone to snatch them out of His hand, either. I and My Father are one."

This angered the Jews so much that they went and got stones to hurl at Him. When they returned, Jesus asked, "I've shown you plenty of good works as evidence from My Father. Which of those works has made you want to stone Me?"

They answered, "It's not because of any good work, but for blasphemy; because you are just a man, and you're making yourself God."

Jesus responded, "Isn't it written in your own Law, 'I said, you are gods'? If He called the ones the Word of God came to gods, and this Scripture, like all others, cannot be broken; how can you say that the One Who God sanctified and sent into the world is blaspheming, because I said, 'I am the Son of God'?" If I am not doing My Father's works, stop believing Me. But since I am doing those works, even if you don't believe Me, at least believe the works: so that you might come to believe that the Father is in Me, and I am in the Father."

Again they tried to seize Him, but He simply walked away out of their hands.

*   *   *

Jesus left the Holy City and crossed to the east side of the Jordan River to Perea, which was the scene of the beginning of the ministry of John the Baptist. Many people came to Him, saying, "John didn't perform any miracles, but everything he said about this man was true."

Many believed in Him there.

He journeyed through the various cities and villages, teaching as He made His way back towards Jerusalem.

A certain person asked, "Are there only a few that will be saved?"

The Lord said to the crowd, "Make every effort to enter through the narrow gate: because I tell you that many will seek to enter, and won't be able to, when the master of the house rises up, and slams the door shut. Then you'll be left outside knocking on the door, and saying, 'Lord, open the door, at once.' He will answer, 'I don't know who you are, nor where you're from.' Then you'll say, 'we ate and drank in your presence, and you taught in our streets'. But He will say, 'I told you, I don't know who you are, nor where you're from. Depart at once, all you workers of iniquity.' There shall be weeping heard, and gnashing of teeth, in that place outside the house where you will be driven, when you see Abraham, Isaac, and Jacob, and all the prophets, in the Kingdom of God, but you have been thrown out. And they shall come from the east, west, north, and south to sit down and feast in the Kingdom of God. Look, there shall be those who are last who shall be first, and those that are first who shall be last."

*   *   *

Another Sabbath came, and Jesus was again invited to share breakfast in the home of one of the ruling Pharisees, along with other guests. Part of the reason was so that it would be easier for them to watch Him. And, behold, there was a man present who suffered from dropsy. Jesus asked the Pharisees and the experts in the Law of Moses, "Is it lawful to heal on the Sabbath Day, or not?"

They sat in silence. Jesus took hold of him, healed him, and let him go.

He said, "If one of you has a donkey or an ox that falls in a ditch, won't you immediately pull it up, even if it's the Sabbath?"

They were once again unable to respond to His arguments.

He gave a parable to those who had been invited, when He was observing how they were choosing for themselves the best seats at the table.

"Whenever you are invited by someone to a wedding, don't

take the chief place at the table; in case a more honorable man than you has been invited and comes, and the host who invited you both, says, 'let this man have your place', and you slowly and shamefully move to take the lowest seat. But whenever you are invited, go and take the last place, so that the one who invited you will say, 'friend, come up higher!' Then you shall be honored before all who are at the table with you: because everyone who exalts himself will be humbled; and he that humbles himself shall be exalted."

Then Jesus said to the one who had invited Him, "Whenever you give a breakfast or a dinner, don't only call your friends, brethren, relatives, and wealthy neighbors, so that they will then invite you to their home in return. But when you make a banquet, call the poor, disabled, lame, and blind; and you will be blessed, because they can't repay you. Your repayment will come at the time of the resurrection of the just."

After hearing this, one of those eating with Jesus said, "Blessed is the one who shall eat in the Kingdom of God."

Jesus said to him, "A certain man made a great supper and invited many people. When the supper was ready, he sent his servant to tell those who had been invited, 'Come, for everything is ready.' But one after another all asked to be excused. The first said, 'I bought a farm, and I need to go and see it. I beg you to excuse me.' Another said, 'I bought five yoke of oxen, and I'm on my way to examine them. I beg you to excuse me.' Another said, 'I have married a wife, and so I cannot come.'

The servant came back and reported all these things to his master, who became angry. He told his servant, 'Quickly go out into the streets and narrow lanes of the city and bring the poor, disabled, blind, and lame in here.' So the servant did so, and returned to his master, and said, 'Lord, I did what you commanded, and yet there is still more room.' So the master said to him, 'go out immediately into the country roads, and the footpaths alongside the hedges and compel them to come in, so that my house may be filled. I say to you, that not one of those who had been originally invited will taste my dinner'."

CHAPTER 29

As Jesus continued to travel, accompanied by great crowds, He suddenly turned around, and said, "If anyone comes to Me, and does not hate his father, mother, spouse, children, brothers, and sisters, and, yes, even his own life, he cannot be My disciple. And whoever does not pick up and carry his cross, and come after Me, cannot be My disciple.

Which of you who intends to build a tower doesn't, first of all, sit down and figure out the cost, to find out if he has the resources to complete it. Lest perhaps, after laying the foundation, he is not able to finish it, and all those who see it begin to mock, saying, 'this fellow began to build, and didn't have what he needed to finish.' Or what king, preparing to go to war with another, doesn't first consider whether he is able to meet the one coming with 20,000 soldiers with his 10,000. If he doesn't think so, while his adversary is still a great way off, he will send an ambassador and request conditions for peace.

So, in the same way, every one of you who literally does not say goodbye to all he has, cannot be My disciple. Salt is good; but if the salt loses its flavor, how will it be restored? It isn't fit for the land, nor even for the manure pile. Men just throw it out. He who has ears to hear, let him hear."

*　　*　　*

To the surprise of the religious leaders, the tax collectors as well as others they considered sinners crowded close to Jesus because they wanted to hear what He had to say. The Pharisees and Scribes began to murmur and complain to each other, "This man not only welcomes sinners, He even eats with them."

Jesus responded, "What man of you, if he had 100 sheep and lost one, doesn't leave the 99 behind and go to search for that lost one until he finds it? And when he finds it, he lays it upon his shoulders rejoicing. And when he gets home, he calls together his friends and neighbors, and says, 'rejoice with me, because I found my sheep that was lost.' I say to you, there shall be more joy in Heaven over one sinner who repents, than over 99 who don't need to repent.

Or, what woman who has ten silver coins, if she loses one, doesn't light a lamp, sweep the house, and search diligently until she finds it? And when she finds it she calls together her lady friends and neighbors, saying, 'rejoice with me, because I found the silver coin I lost'. Likewise, joy arises in the presence of the holy angels of God over one sinner who repents.

A certain man had two sons. The younger one said to his father, 'father, give me the share of the estate which falls to me'. And he divided his wealth to them. And not many days afterward, the younger son gathered all his possessions, and left his own country to go to a faraway place. There he wasted all he had by living a sinful life of abandon. And after he had squandered it all, there arose a mighty famine in that country, and he began to be in want.

So he went and forced himself on one of the citizens of the

country who really didn't want to hire him. He was sent into the fields to feed swine. He longed to fill his own stomach with the very pods he was giving to the swine, but no one would give him permission. He finally came to his senses, and said, 'how many employees of my father have more bread than they can eat, and here I am starving to death. I will get up and go to my father, and say, Father, I sinned against Heaven, and in your sight; and I'm no longer worthy to be called your son. Please just make me as one of your employees.'

So he got ready, and went to his father. But while he was still a long distance away, his father saw him, was moved with compassion, ran and fell on his neck, tenderly kissing him over and over again. The son said to him, 'Father, I sinned against Heaven, and in your sight, and I'm no longer worthy to be called your son.' But the father yelled to the servants, 'Quickly, bring out the finest robe in the house, and put it on him. And put a ring on his hand, and sandals on his feet. Then bring out the fatted calf that we save for joyous occasions, and kill it; and let's eat, and be merry: because this son of mine, who was dead, is alive again. He was lost, but has been found'. And they began to be merry.

Now his older son had been in the field working; and when he came near the house, he heard musicians playing, and the sound of people dancing. He called one of the servants to ask what was happening. He said to him, 'Your brother returned, and your father has killed the fatted calf because he got him back safe and sound.'The older brother flew into a rage and refused to go into the house. So the father came out and pleaded with him.

He answered his father, 'Look. For years I have served you, and never once broke your rules: and you never even gave me a young goat, so that my friends and I could make merry. But as soon as this son of yours, who devoured your money with prostitutes, comes, you kill the fatted calf for him.'

His father answered, 'Son, you are always with me, and all

my things are yours. But it was right to celebrate and be glad: because this brother of yours was dead, and is alive again; he was lost, and is found.'"

Now Jesus turned his attention to His disciples: "There was a certain rich man who had a steward managing his estate, who was found to be wasting the master's goods.

So he called the man in, and said, 'what is this that I hear about you? I want you to give me a report this very moment about the way you've been managing my estate; because you can no longer be my steward.'

The steward said to himself, 'What am I going to do now that my master is taking away my position? I'm not strong enough to dig, and I'm too proud to beg. I have it! I'll do something that will cause people to welcome me into their homes when I'm officially removed from my position.'

One by one he called in each of those who owed money to his master.

He said to the first, 'How much do you owe my master?'

'100 measures of oil.'

The steward said, 'Here take your bill, sit down quickly, and make it 50.'

He called in another, 'How much do you owe?'

'100 measures of wheat.'

'Here, take your bill at once and make it 80'; and so on he went.

When his master heard what he had done he praised the unjust steward, because he acted shrewdly. The children of this world are shrewder in dealing with their own kind than the sons of light are with theirs. I say unto you, make yourselves friends by using unrighteous riches, so that when those riches fail, the friends you make by your generosity may welcome you into eternal dwelling places. He who proves to be faithful in very little will prove to be faithful also in much; and he who is unjust in a very little thing will be the same in much.

If, therefore, you weren't faithful in riches that are

considered unrighteous, who will entrust you with true riches? And if you weren't faithful with what belongs to someone else, who will give you your own riches. No servant can serve two masters: for either he will hate one and love the other, or he will hold firmly to one and despise the other. You cannot go on trying to serve God and riches."

The Pharisees, who loved money, were listening to all these things and began to ridicule Him. He said to them, "You are the ones who claim to be righteous before men. But God knows your hearts, and that which is highly esteemed by men makes God sick. The Law and the Prophets were until John the Baptist. Since that time, the good news of the Kingdom of God is being preached and everyone with passion and energy strives to go in and be a part of it. And it's easier for Heaven and Earth to perish than for the tiniest part of the Law to fail. Everyone who dismisses his wife and marries another commits adultery. And he who marries her who has been dismissed from her husband commits adultery.

Now there was a certain rich man who always clothed himself in purple and fine linen and ate lavishly every day. And there was a certain beggar named Lazarus who they just threw down carelessly at his gate where he stayed, covered with ulcers and sores. He eagerly desired to be fed the crumbs which he watched falling from time to time from the rich man's table. And the dogs came and licked his sores.

It came to pass that the beggar died and was carried by the angels to be with Abraham in Paradise. And the rich man also died and was buried. He found himself in hell where he lifted up his eyes, being in torment, and he could see Abraham afar off, and Lazarus with him in Paradise.

He cried out, 'Father Abraham, have mercy on me, and quickly send Lazarus, so that he may dip the tip of his finger in water, and cool off my tongue, because I am in agony because of these flames.'

Abraham said, 'Child, remember that you received your

good things in your lifetime, and Lazarus likewise evil things. But now in this place he is comforted, but you are in anguish. And besides all this, there is a great chasm that has been put permanently in place so that those who want to cross over to you cannot, and likewise those who want to pass over from there to us cannot.'

Then he said, 'Then, I beg of you, father Abraham, to send him to my father's house: for I have five brothers; so that they might not also come to this place of torment.'

Abraham replied, 'They have Moses and the Prophets; let them hear them.'

But he said, 'They won't, father Abraham: but if someone went from the dead, they would. Then they would listen and repent.'

Abraham replied, 'Since they don't listen to Moses and the Prophets, even if someone was to rise from the dead, they will not be persuaded.'"

Then Jesus said to His disciples, "It is impossible for anyone to say that stumbling blocks will not come. But woe to that person through whom they come. It is more profitable for him to have a millstone hung around his neck and that he be hurled into the sea, than that he would cause one of these little ones to stumble. Take heed to yourselves. If your brother sins against you, rebuke him at once. If he repents, forgive him. In fact, if he sins against you seven times in a day, and all seven times returns to you saying, 'I'm sorry', forgive him."

The Apostles said to the Lord, "Lord, increase our faith."

He said, "If you had faith like a grain of mustard seed, you would say to this tree, 'be uprooted and planted in the sea', and it would obey you. But which of you having a servant who is plowing or tending to a flock of sheep, when he has come in from the field will say to him, 'go ahead, sit down and have something to eat.'

Instead, won't he say, 'Prepare at once something for me to eat, put on some clean clothes and wait on me till I eat and drink, and after that you get something to eat and drink'. He doesn't thank the servant for doing the things he was commanded to do, does he?

So likewise, when you have done all the things which you were commanded to do, say, 'We are servants who have done nothing more than we were commanded to do. We don't deserve any credit, because all we did was what we were supposed to do'."

CHAPTER 30

While Jesus' ministry in Perea continued, back in Bethany, Lazarus, the brother of Martha and Mary, became very ill. The sisters sent a messenger to find the Lord and let Him know. When the servant found Jesus, he told Him, "Lord, I was sent to tell you, the one who you love is sick."

After hearing this, the Lord said, "Go back and tell Martha and Mary that this sickness is not going to end in death. It is for the glory of God and the Son of God is going to be glorified."

But instead of going to Bethany, Jesus remained in Perea and Lazarus got worse and worse until he finally died.

The Lord told the Apostles, "Let us go into Judea again."

They reminded Him, "Master, are you sure you want to go back there, because the Jews were just now seeking to stone you?"

"Aren't there twelve hours of daytime? If a person walks about in the day he doesn't stumble or bump into anything, because he sees the light of the world. But if he walks in the night he stumbles, because there is no light in him. Our friend Lazarus has fallen asleep, but I'm going there so that I can wake him up."

His disciples said, "Lord, if he fell asleep, that's a good thing, and it will help him recover."

When the Lord realized that they thought He meant actual sleep, he told them plainly, "Lazarus is dead. And I'm glad for your sakes that I wasn't there, so that you may believe. But now let's go to him."

Then Thomas said to his fellow disciples, "Let us also go, so that we may die with Him."

Since Bethany was only two miles east of Jerusalem on the southeast slope of the Mount of Olives, many friends and loved ones came to console Martha and Mary. While some helped prepare the mourning meal, others simply sat silently on the ground with the grieving sisters. When the time came, they all joined the procession that followed the body of Lazarus out to the tomb. After the burial, when they arrived back at the grieving home, they formed two lines outside. The two sisters walked through the midst of them as they heard their loved ones and friends speak words of sympathy until they finally entered their home. The thirty days of bereavement officially began.

By the time Jesus arrived in Bethany, Lazarus had been in the tomb for four days. Before He even reached the home of Mary and Martha, He was recognized and word came to the house announcing that he was coming. Martha went out to meet Him as soon as she heard, but Mary remained in the house.

When she finally found Jesus, she said, "Lord, if you had been here my brother would not have died. But even now I'm sure that whatever you ask God, He will give it to you."

Jesus said, "Your brother will rise again."

She replied, "I'm sure that he will rise again in the resurrection on the last day."

Jesus said, "I am the Resurrection and the Life. He who

believes in Me shall live even if he dies. And whoever lives and believes in Me shall never die. Do you believe this?"

She said, "Yes, Lord. I believe that you are the Christ, the Son of God, Who was to come into the world."

She left and went back to her home where she secretly told Mary, "The Master is here and is calling for you."

When Mary heard that, she quickly got up and went to find Him. The people who were in the house consoling her saw that, and followed her, supposing that she was going to the tomb to weep there. Jesus hadn't reached the village yet, but was still where Martha had found Him. When Mary arrived where He was and saw Him, she fell at His feet and through her tears said, "Lord, if you had been here my brother wouldn't have died."

When the Lord saw her weeping, as well as the Jews who had come with her, He groaned in His spirit and was deeply troubled.

Then He said, "Where have you laid him?"

They said, "Come and see."

As he followed, He burst into tears and wept silently.

The Jews said, "Look how much He loved him."

Others said, "Couldn't this man, who opened the eyes of the blind, have kept this man from dying?"

Jesus again groaned with exasperation as He came to the grave. It was a cave with a stone laid against it.

He said, "Take away the stone."

Martha, being the sister of the deceased, said, "Lord, by this time there is going to be a horrible odor, for he has been dead for four days."

Jesus said, "Didn't I say that if you would believe, you would see the glory of God."

Then they took away the stone from where the dead man was laid. Jesus lifted up His eyes, and prayed, "Father, I thank you, because you heard Me. And I know that you always hear Me, but because of the crowd standing here I said that, so that they may believe that you sent Me."

After saying these things, Jesus raised His voice and shouted, "Lazarus, come out."

At once the dead man came hobbling out, bound securely around his hands and feet with grave clothes, with a handkerchief bound around his face.

Jesus said, "Untie him at once and let him go."

Many of the Jews, who came with Mary and had seen what He did, believed in Him. But some of them went off to the Pharisees and told them what Jesus had done.

*   *   *

The chief priests and Pharisees convened a council, and said, "What are we doing? This man is performing countless miracles? If we leave Him alone about this, everyone will believe in Him, and the Romans will come and take away both our place and our nation."

One of them, Caiaphas, who was high priest, said to them, "You don't know anything at all. Nor do you consider that it is in your best interest that one man should die for the people, instead of the whole nation being destroyed."

He didn't speak these words from himself, but since he was the High Priest that year he was actually prophesying that Jesus would die for the nation; but not only for that nation, but that the children of God which had been scattered abroad should be gathered into one by Him.

From that day forward, they took counsel together about how to put Him to death, and so He no longer walked about openly among the Jews. He traveled northeast into the country near the wilderness to the city of Ephraim, which was 16 miles away, located on a hill overlooking the Jordan Valley, where he stayed with His Apostles.

*   *   *

The Jewish Passover was near and many people came from all over Palestine and many other parts of the world, so that they could ceremonially purify themselves before the Feast. The Chief Priests and Pharisees had given the command that if anyone knew where Jesus was that he should disclose it so that they might arrest Him. There were those who had begun to watch for Him, and as they stood in the Temple they discussed the situation.

"What do you think? There is absolutely no way He would dare come to the Feast."

But Jesus was surely coming, because His hour had finally come. He was already making His way toward Jerusalem. He left Ephraim, and was going through the midst of Samaria and Galilee, planning to cross over the Jordan near Bethshean to join the Galilean Caravan going down through Perea to the Holy City.

As He was entering a village, He was met by a group of ten lepers standing at distance, as the Law of Moses required. They lifted up their voices and cried out, "Jesus, Master, have mercy on us, and help us."

When He saw them, He said, "Go and show yourselves as proof to the Priests."

They did as they were told and had not gone very far when they realized they had been healed. One of them, a Samaritan, immediately turned back and could be heard from a distance glorifying God. He fell down on his face at the feet of Jesus, thanking Him.

The Lord said, "Weren't there ten cleansed? Where are the other nine? None of them returned to give glory to God, except this foreigner."

Then he said to the man, "Arise and be on your way. Your faith made you whole."

He continued on His journey and was met by some Pharisees who demanded to be told when the Kingdom of God would come.

Jesus answered, "The Kingdom of God doesn't come in a way that can be observed. Neither shall they say, 'look, it's here', or, 'it's there'; because, see, the Kingdom of God is in the very midst of you."

Then He said to His disciples, "The days will come when you will long to see one of the days of the Son of Man, and shall not see it. And they shall say to you, 'Look there in that place. Look here.' Don't follow after them; for just as the lightning suddenly flashes from one point under Heaven to the other, so shall the Son of Man be in His day. But first He must suffer many things, and be rejected by this generation.

As it was in the days of Noah, so it shall also be in the days of the Son of Man. They were eating, drinking, marrying, and being given in marriage, until the day Noah entered the Ark. Then the Flood came and destroyed them all. It will also be like it was in the days of Lot. They were eating, drinking, buying, selling, planting, and building. But on the very day Lot went out of Sodom, it rained fire and brimstone from Heaven and destroyed them all. That is the way it will be on the day when the Son of Man is revealed.

On that day, if someone is on his housetop while his possessions are in the house, let him not go down to get them. And he who is in the field, likewise, don't let him return to the things he left behind. Remember Lot's wife. Whoever shall seek to preserve his life will lose it, and whoever shall lose his life shall preserve it.

I tell you, on that night there shall be two in one bed: the one shall be taken, and the other shall be left. There shall be two women grinding at the same place: the one shall be taken, and the other left. Two men shall be in the field: the one shall be taken, and the other left."

They asked, "Where, Lord?"

He answered, "Where the carcass is, there the vultures will be gathered together."

Jesus gave them a parable to make the point that it was necessary for men to always keep on praying, and not to lose heart.

"There was a certain judge, in a certain city, that didn't fear God, and had no respect for anyone. Now there was a widow in that city who kept on coming back to him again and again, saying, 'Give me justice from my opponent in a lawsuit.' He refused to help her for a long time, but afterward he said to himself, 'although I don't fear God and don't respect anyone, I will see that this woman gets justice because she keeps on bothering me. Otherwise she might finally try to physically harm me.'

Did you hear what the unjust judge said? Shall not God vindicate His Own elect, who cry out day and night to Him, even though He delays that help? I tell you, He will give them justice speedily. Yet when the Son of Man comes, will He find the kind of faith the widow had, which made her so persistent?"

CHAPTER 31

The day came when Jesus found Himself in a conversation with some people who were convinced that they themselves were worthy and righteous, while despising everyone else. He shared this parable:

"Two men went up to the Temple to pray; one was a Pharisee, and the other a tax collector. The Pharisee made sure to stand where everyone could see him and began to pray, saying to himself, 'O God, I am thankful to you that I am not like the rest of mankind, who are extortioners, unjust, adulterers, or even like that tax collector over there. I fast twice a week, and I pay a tenth of all my income to the Temple.'

But the tax collector stood at a distance from the Pharisee, and refused to even lift up his eyes to Heaven, but kept on beating his breast, saying, 'O God, be merciful to me the sinner.' I tell you, this man went down to his house declared righteous, rather than that other one. For everyone who exalts himself will be abased, and he who humbles himself will be exalted."

When Jesus had finished these sayings, He departed from Galilee and came into the regions of Judea, and then crossed the Jordan. There were crowds again journeying with Him, who were constantly coming to Him to be taught and healed.

The Pharisees came to Him and kept asking over and over again, "Is it lawful for a man to dismiss a wife for every cause?", trying to put Him to a test.

He finally answered, "What did Moses command you about this?"

They said, "Moses allowed us to write a bill of divorce, and then dismiss her."

Jesus answered, "Haven't you read that the Creator from the very beginning made them male and female, and on account of this a man shall leave his father and mother to be joined to his wife, and the two shall be one flesh? Therefore they are no longer two, but one flesh. So that which God yoked together once and for all, don't let man separate."

They asked, "Then why did Moses command to give a bill of divorcement and dismiss her?"

Jesus explained, "Because of the hardness of your hearts, Moses allowed you to dismiss your wives. But from the beginning, the right to divorce has not been, and that has never changed. Moreover, I tell you, whoever dismisses his wife for any cause other than fornication, and marries another, commits adultery. And whoever marries her that was put away commits adultery."

Later when they returned to the house they were staying in, the disciples said to Him, "If what you said about marriage is true, it's better not to marry."

He explained, "Not all receive this word with understanding, except those who have been given the ability to understand it. For there are some who are eunuchs who were born that way from their mother's womb; and there are some who were made eunuchs by men. And there are some who have made themselves eunuchs for the sake of the Kingdom of Heaven. He who is able to receive this with understanding, let him receive it."

*   *   *

As Jesus was preparing to leave, mothers approached the house with their babies and little children, hoping that He would touch them and pray for them. But when the disciples saw this they stopped them and rebuked them. Jesus saw what was happening, and became angry, and began to call the children to come to Him.

He told His disciples, "Permit the children to come to Me. Don't forbid them. For ones such as these shall have the Kingdom of Heaven."

As He began to pick the children up in His arms to bless them, He added, "I assure you, whoever doesn't receive the Kingdom of Heaven as a little child does, shall absolutely not enter it."

When Jesus finally finished blessing the children, He left the house and began to walk up the road, when someone came running towards Him. It was a young ruler who fell on his knees before Him, and asked, "Good Master, what good thing should I do, so that I may inherit eternal life?"

The Lord answered, "Why are you calling Me good? The only One Who is good is God. But since you want to enter into eternal life, keep the Commandments."

"Which ones?"

"You shall not murder, you shall not commit adultery, you shall not steal, you shall not bear false witness, do not defraud, honor your father and your mother, and you shall love your neighbor as yourself."

He answered, "I have kept all these things since I was a boy. What do I still lack?"

As Jesus looked at this young man, he lovingly said, "You do lack one thing. If you want to be perfect, go, sell all your belongings and give to the poor, and you will have treasure in Heaven. Then come, take up your cross, and follow Me."

When he heard this he was saddened, and his face filled with gloom. He walked away grieved, because he was very wealthy. As the Lord watched him walk sorrowfully away, He looked around at His disciples, and said, "How difficult it is for someone who is wealthy to enter the Kingdom of Heaven."

The Apostles were astonished at this, and Jesus went further: "How difficult it is for those who trust in their riches to enter the Kingdom of Heaven. It's easier for a camel to go through the eye of a sewing needle, than for a rich man to enter the Kingdom of Heaven."

Now they were almost beside themselves with amazement, and cried to one another, "Then, who can be saved?"

Jesus looked at them and said, "With men it's impossible, but not with God; for with God all things are possible."

Peter asked, "Behold, we have forsaken all, and followed you. What will there be for us?"

Jesus answered, "I assure you, you who have followed Me, that when all things are restored to their original glory and the Son of Man shall sit down on His glorious throne, you shall also sit down upon twelve thrones, judging the twelve tribes of Israel.

I assure you, there is no one who has abandoned house, or brothers, or sisters, or parents, or wife, or children, for My sake and the sake of the Gospel, who shall not receive one hundred times as much at this time, houses, brothers, sisters, mothers, children, and lands, with persecution, and in the world to come, eternal life. But many who are first shall be last, and the last ones, first.

For the Kingdom of Heaven is like a man who was the master of a house, who went out at daybreak to hire workers for his vineyard. When he had agreed with some workers for a denarius a day, he sent them into the vineyard to work. Then he went out again at nine AM, and saw others standing around in the market place, unemployed, and said to them, 'You go into my vineyard too, and whatever is right, I will give you', and they did so.

He went out again at noon, and three PM, and did the same thing.

Finally, about Five PM he went out and found others just standing around, and said to them, 'Why have you stood here all day long doing nothing?'

They replied, 'Because no one hired us.'

He said, 'You go into the vineyard as well, and whatever is right, you'll receive.'

When evening came, the master of the vineyard told his manager, 'Call the workers together now and give them their pay, beginning with the last ones hired to those who were the first.'

When those who were hired at Five PM came, they received a denarius. But when those who had been hired first finally came to be paid, they supposed they would receive more, but they also received a denarius. When they received it, they began to grumble and complain against the master of the house, muttering, 'These last ones only worked for an hour, and you made them equal to us who bore the burden of the whole day along with its scorching heat.'

But the master answered the one who had come representing the ones who were upset, 'Friend, I'm not treating you unjustly. Didn't you agree to work for one denarius? Take what's yours and go on your way. I want to give the last ones the same amount I gave you. Can't I do what I want with what is mine? Or does this show that your eye is evil because I am generous?' So the last shall be first, and the first last; for many are called, but few are chosen."

*   *   *

Jesus and His men continued to make their way up to Jerusalem. He walked out ahead of them with a determination that astonished them, and as they traveled on they began to be afraid. So He took the twelve apart from everyone else to talk privately to them about what was about to take place.

"Look! We are going up to Jerusalem, and all the things that were written by the prophets concerning the Son of Man shall be accomplished. He shall be betrayed into the hands of the Chief Priests and Scribes, and condemned to death. Then they'll hand Him over to the Gentiles to be mocked, shamefully treated, and spit on. Then they'll scourge Him and, finally, crucify Him. And on the third day He will rise again."

They didn't understand any of this. This word was completely hidden from them, so they didn't comprehend what was being said at all.

The mother of the sons of Zebedee came to Him with her sons, falling on her knees and touching the ground with her forehead to show reverence, and requested permission to ask Him for something.

Jesus said, "What do you want?"

She said, "Grant that my two sons may sit, one on your right hand, and one on your left, in your glory."

"You don't know what you're asking for? Are you able to drink from the cup that I'm about to drink from, and to be baptized with the baptism I am to be baptized with?"

They confidently claimed, "We are able."

"You shall indeed drink from My cup, and be baptized with the baptism I'm to be baptized with. But to sit on My right hand and on my left isn't mine to give, but it is for those for whom it is prepared by My Father."

When the other ten heard this conversation, they were angry and resentful at the two brothers. So Jesus called them to Him, and said, "You know that the rulers of the Gentiles rule with absolute power over them, and the great ones are like tyrants who dominate them. That's not the way it is to be with you.

Whoever wants to be great, shall be your servant; and whoever wants to be the greatest of all, must be the servant of all. For even the Son of Man didn't come to be served but to serve, and to give His life as a ransom for many."

CHAPTER 32

For the last time, Jesus crossed the Jordan River and entered Judea. They passed through ancient Jericho on their way to Roman Jericho, and as they were departing they passed by two blind men sitting by the wayside, begging.

The blind men heard the sound of the crowds passing by and asked several of the people what was happening, and someone finally told them, "Jesus of Nazareth is passing by."

When they heard this, they immediately began to shout, "Jesus, Son of David, have mercy on us."

Those who were passing by rebuked them sharply and told them to be quiet, but instead they cried out even more, "Jesus, Son of David, have mercy on us."

Jesus stopped and commanded that the blind men be brought to Him. So they called them and said to them, "Be of good courage; come, He's calling you."

They threw off their outer robes, leaped to their feet, and hurried to Jesus. When they came near, He asked them, "What do you want Me to do for you?"

The one named Bartimaeus said, "Rabboni, that our eyes may be opened, and we can see again."

So Jesus had compassion on them, touched their eyes, and said, "Receive your sight. Go your way; your faith has made you whole."

Immediately they received their sight and began to follow Him, glorifying God; and when all the people saw what had happened, they praised Him as well.

*   *   *

After the brief pause, the crowd continued on towards Roman Jericho. As they approached, they could see the walls flanked by four forts that had been built by Herod the Great. As they passed through the city gates, they could see the theater and amphitheater, also built by the same Herod, as well as the new palace built by his son, Archelaus, which was surrounded by beautiful gardens.

The streets were crowded with travelers from Galilee and Perea, as well as traders from all over the world who were taking the great caravan road from Arabia and Damascus, and also with Roman soldiers and countless others. And tax collectors seemed to be everywhere, especially since Jericho was the central station for collecting taxes and customs.

One of the chief tax collectors was a man named Zacchaeus, who had made himself wealthy by overcharging Israelite tax payers. As the throngs of people entered the city, he tried to figure out which one of these was the Jesus he had heard so much about, but he couldn't because the crowd was so large and he was so small. He decided to run on ahead and climb a sycamore tree that he realized the crowd was going to pass beneath. Perhaps then he might get a look at the Rabbi from Nazareth. As Jesus came up to the tree, He looked up and saw the tax collector.

He said, "Zacchaeus, hurry down, because today I need to be a guest in your house."

So he hurried down, rejoicing, and welcomed Him as his guest.

When the crowd saw this, they murmured to one another, complaining, "He has gone to be the guest of a man who is a notorious sinner."

The murmuring continued all the way to the home of Zacchaeus. So before entering he stopped, turned around, and while facing the crowd, he said to the Lord, "Behold, half of my possessions I am going to give to the poor; and whatever I have taken by false accusation from anyone, I will now restore four times as much."

Jesus said to him, "Today salvation has come to this house, because he himself is also a son of Abraham; for the Son of Man has come to seek and to save that which was lost."

While the people were listening to this, Jesus added a parable because He was near Jerusalem, and there were some who were under the impression that the Kingdom of God would immediately appear.

"A certain nobleman went off to a distant country to receive a kingdom for himself, planning to return. He called his ten servants, gave them ten pounds of money, and said, 'Trade and do business until I return.' But his citizens hated him and sent a government representative after him, who said, 'We don't want this man to reign as king over us.'

It came to pass that when he returned after receiving the kingdom, he commanded the servants who had been given the money to be brought to him, so that he might find out how much each had gained by trading.

The first one approached and said, 'Master, your pound has been invested and has earned ten pounds more.'

The master said, 'Well done, good servant. Because you were faithful in a small thing, have authority over ten cities.'

The second one came, saying, 'Master, your pound has been

invested and earned five pounds more.'

And he said to this one, 'You be over five cities.'

And then another came to him, and said, 'Master, look, here's your pound that I have held onto for you in this handkerchief. I was afraid of you because you are a hard and austere man who has a habit of profiting from what you didn't deposit, and reaping what you didn't sow.'

The master said, 'Out of your own mouth I will judge you, wicked servant. Did you know that I was a hard and austere man, profiting from what I didn't deposit, and reaping from what I didn't sow? In that case, why didn't you put my money in the bank, so that I would at least have gotten my money back with interest?'

He said to those who were standing by, 'Take the pound from him, and give it to the one who has the ten pounds.'

They said to him, 'Master, he already has ten pounds.'

He told them, 'To everyone who has, more shall be given; and from the one who does not have, even what he has will be taken. But those enemies who didn't want me to reign over them as king, bring them here and slaughter them in front of me.'"

Jesus then resumed His journey up the hill towards the Holy City, followed by the multitude.

*   *   *

Friday afternoon, before sunset when the Sabbath began, Jesus arrived in Bethany where Lazarus, who He raised from the dead, lived. When the common people among the Jews found out that He was there, they came to see Him, as well as Lazarus himself. Because of this friend of Jesus, many withdrew from the Jewish leadership and began to believe in Jesus. The chief priests consulted together about how to kill him, as well.

*   *   *

On Sunday, after the Sabbath had ended, Jesus and His disciples left Bethany and walked up a steep hill, and a short time later arrived at the top near Bethpage. Here Jesus gave Peter and another of the Apostles a surprising order.

"Go into the village opposite you. As soon as you enter it, you'll find a donkey tied up and a colt with her that no one has ever ridden. Untie them and bring them here to me. If anyone says, 'Why are you loosing them?', just say, 'The Lord needs them, and will be sure to return them'; and they will immediately send them."

They went off and found the animals tied to a door outside in an open winding road, and began to untie them. One of those who owned them who was standing there, said, "What are you doing loosing the donkey and its colt?"

The disciples replied just as Jesus told them to, and were given permission. They brought the animals back to where the Lord was, and began to throw their own outer garments on the colt for Jesus to sit on. As they began to travel, many people began to spread their outer garments into the road, and others cut branches and leaves from nearby fields and laid them in the road as well.

Word reached Jerusalem, "Jesus is coming into the city," and people began to pick up palm branches and went out to meet Him.

When the throng that accompanied Jesus met the crowds coming out of Jerusalem, witnesses of the raising of Lazarus began to testify to others of the miracle. They all began to praise God for this, as well as all the mighty works they had seen. They cried out, "Hosanna. Blessed is He Who comes in the Name of the Lord."

As they began the descent, they caught the first sight of Mount Zion, and the southeastern corner of the city, which rose terrace upon terrace from the Palace of the Maccabees and the High Priest, till it reached the summit where Herod's palace with its magnificent garden was.

The multitude then began to cry out, "Blessed be the Kingdom of our Father David and the king who comes in the Name of the Lord. Peace in Heaven and glory in the Highest."

Some of the Pharisees, when they heard what the crowd was saying, said to Him, "Teacher, rebuke your disciples at once."

Jesus pointed at the stones strewn on the road, and said, "If these people were silent, those stones would cry out."

As He continued on, the Pharisees said to one another, "Do you realize you're not doing anything helpful to us. Look! The whole world has gone after Him."

The procession continued to descend, with the city temporarily blocked by the ridge of the Mount of Olives. They reached a rise that led to a ledge of smooth rock, and there it was. The entire city of Jerusalem burst into view, as Jesus burst into tears.

As He wept, He said, "If only you had known in this day, the things tending to your peace. But now they have been hidden from your eyes. For the days will come upon you when your enemies will throw up a rampart before you, encircle you, and hold you in on every side. And they shall level you and dash you to the ground, both you and your children in you, and not leave one stone upon another. And all of this is because you didn't recognize this visitation of God's care and offer to help."

When the Lord finally entered Jerusalem, the city was shaken, and the people asked, "Who is this?"

The crowds said over and over, "This is Jesus, the prophet from Nazareth of Galilee."

He went to the Temple and carefully looked around at the porches, courts, and outer buildings and eventually left the city with the Twelve, and returned that night to Bethany.

*　　*　　*

Very early the next morning they left Bethany, and Jesus

was hungry. He saw a lone fig tree a long way off by the road, with leaves on it. Even though it wasn't the season of figs, He assumed that He might find some because of the leaves, since they normally appeared after the fruit had grown. But when He finally reached the tree He found that it didn't have anything but leaves.

His disciples overheard Him say to the tree, "Not one person will ever eat fruit from you again."

*   *   *

The Lord and His Apostles entered Jerusalem and went directly to the Temple where He had only gone and observed the day before. They entered the Court of the Gentiles, which was the outer enclosure of the Sanctuary made up of a huge 750 foot square of the finest variegated marble. The place was filled with the sights, sounds, and smells of the sheep, oxen, and other animals that were being sold for sacrifice. Men sat at tables, exchanging different currencies into the Temple money needed to purchase an animal, or pay the Temple tax.

Christ shocked everyone by beginning to throw down the tables of the money changers, scattering coins everywhere, and the seats of those who were selling animals. He chased out all those who were buying and selling anything in the Court, and refused to allow anyone to use the Temple as a shortcut for carrying things here and there.

A crowd gathered to see what was happening and Jesus began to teach them, "Isn't it written, 'My house shall be called a house of prayer for all nations'? But you have made it a den of thieves."

Blind people and others who were maimed in various ways approached the Lord and he healed them.

Then little children, who were witnessing all this, began crying out there in the Temple, "Hosanna to the Son of David;" which enraged the chief priests and scribes.

They said to Jesus, "Do you hear what these are saying?"

He replied, "Yes. Haven't you ever read, 'Out of the mouth of infants and little ones who are nursing you have perfected praise'?"

*   *   *

That evening, Jesus left the city and returned to Bethany and lodged there. In the meanwhile, the scribes, chief priests, and leaders of the people sought unsuccessfully for a way to destroy Him; because they feared Him because of the multitude who were struck with astonishment by His teaching, and hung on His every word.

*   *   *

Some Greeks who had come up to the Feast to worship came to Philip, and said, "Sir, we would like to have the chance to speak with Jesus."

Philip told Andrew of their request, and the two of them went to tell Jesus.

He said, "The hour has come that the Son of Man should be glorified. I assure you, unless a grain of wheat falls into the ground and dies, it remains alone. But if it dies, it bears much fruit. He that loves his life shall lose it. And he who hates his life in this world, and chooses eternal life instead, shall save it. If any man serves Me, let him make a habit of following Me, so that where I am My servant will be there also. If anyone serves Me, My Father will honor him. Now My soul is troubled. So what shall I say, 'Father, rescue Me from this hour'?

It is because of this I have come to this hour. Father, glorify Your Name."

Then a voice was heard from Heaven, "I have glorified it, and will glorify it again."

The crowd that was standing nearby and heard the voice,

said, "That was the sound of thunder."

But others said, "An angel spoke to Him."

Jesus answered, "It is not for My sake that this voice came, but for yours. Now is this world judged. Now the ruler of this world will be completely thrown out. And when I am lifted up from the earth, I will draw all men to Me."

He said this to show what kind of death He was to die.

So the crowd answered, "We have heard out of the Law that the Christ lives and abides forever. How is it that you say it is necessary for the Son of Man to be lifted up? Who is this Son of Man?"

Jesus said, "The light is among you a little while longer. Walk while you still have the light, so that the darkness doesn't overtake you; because the one who walks in darkness doesn't know where he is going. While you have the light, believe in the light, so that you may be children of the light.

CHAPTER 33

The Pharisees deliberated with one another about how they might trap Jesus by something He said. They knew that there were Roman soldiers from the Fortress Antonia, which was located on the northwest corner of the Temple complex, stationed throughout the area. They would position themselves behind the columns that encircled the perimeter of the Temple and listen to the conversations going on, just in case they heard something that represented a threat to Rome. The Jewish leaders hoped they could get Jesus to say something that would cause Him to be arrested and taken before Pontius Pilate, the Roman Governor.

Some of the students of the Pharisees, accompanied by supporters of King Herod, were sent to Jesus; they were to act like honest men, but were actually spies who were to try to catch Him in something He said.

They said, "Master, we know that you always speak the truth, that you always teach what is right, and that you are not influenced by who you are talking to, but always teach the ways of God truthfully. Tell us whether you think it's allowed by God's Law for us to pay taxes to Caesar, or not. Should we give, or not?"

Jesus recognized their cunning and wickedness, and said, "You hypocrites, why do you test Me? Bring Me the coin you use to pay the tribute."

When they brought it to Him, He asked, "Whose image and title is on it?"

They answered, "Caesar's."

He replied, "Pay to Caesar the things that are Caesar's; and give to God the things that are God's."

They marveled at His answer, and walked away in silence. Then some of the Sadducees approached the Lord with a question. They were completely against the idea that there is such a thing as a resurrection.

"Teacher, Moses wrote unto us, if any man's brother dies, leaving a wife but no children, that his brother should take his wife and raise up offspring for his brother. Now there were seven brothers with us. The first took a wife, and died, having no children. Then the second took her, but also died childless, and the third also. In the same manner, all seven had her, and died childless. Last of all, the woman died also. Therefore, in the Resurrection, whose wife will she be, since all seven had her?"

Jesus responded, "You are in error because you are ignorant of the Scriptures and of the power of God. The children of this age marry and are given in marriage. But they that rise from the dead don't marry, nor do they give in marriage, and also can't die anymore; but in these respects are like the angels. They are the children of God, since they are the sons of the Resurrection.

Now to show you that the dead are raised, didn't you read in the Book of Moses how God spoke to him at the bush, and said, 'I am the God of Abraham, the God of Isaac, and the God of

Jacob?' He is not the God of dead people, but of the living: for all live with respect to Him. Therefore you are in great error."

When the multitude heard this they were astonished by His teaching, and certain of the Scribes said, "Teacher, you have answered exquisitely."

As the Pharisees heard them reasoning together, and knowing that He had answered well and silenced the Sadducees, one of them, who was a lawyer, tested Him by asking Him a question. "Teacher, what is the first and great commandment of the Law?"

He answered, "The first of all the commandments is, 'Hear, O Israel; the Lord our God is One Lord: and you shall love the Lord your God with your whole heart, with your whole soul, with your whole mind, and with all your strength.' This is the first and great commandment, and the second is this, 'You shall love your neighbor as yourself.' There is none other commandment greater than these. On these two commandments hang all the Law and the Prophets."

The Scribe said, "Exactly! Well said! Teacher, what you said is the truth: for there is One God; and there is none other but He: and to love Him with your whole heart, and with your whole understanding, and with all your strength, and to love your neighbor as yourself, is much more than all the whole burnt offerings and sacrifices."

When Jesus saw that he answered intelligently, He said to him, "You are not far from the Kingdom of Heaven."

After this, no one dared to ask Him about anything, but while the Pharisees were gathered there together, Jesus asked them a question: "How is it that the Scribes say that the Messiah is David's Son? For David himself said in the Book of Psalms by the Holy Spirit, 'The Lord said to My Lord, sit on My right hand, till I make your enemies your footstool'. David himself calls Him Lord, so how can He be his Son?"

No one was able to give Him an answer, and the crowd of common people heard Him gladly. While all the people were listening, Jesus said to His disciples, "Beware of the Scribes and the Pharisees. They sit in Moses' seat, so whatever they tell you to observe, observe and do; but don't do what they do. They are always saying, and not doing. They always bind heavy burdens and put them on men's shoulders, but they don't move them with one finger. They love to parade around in long stately robes, and make their tassels larger, and make their phylacteries broad. But they only do this so that they will be seen and admired by men. And they love the most prominent places at banquets and dinners, and the chief seats in the synagogues, and being greeted with reverence in the markets, and to be called, Rabbi, by men.

Don't seek to be called Rabbi; for Christ is your one Teacher, and you all are brothers. Don't call any man on earth your father, for He Who is in Heaven is your Father. Don't be called master, because the Christ is your one Master. But he who is greatest among you shall be your servant: and whoever shall exalt himself shall be humbled; and whoever shall humble himself shall be exalted.

Woe unto you, scribes and Pharisees, hypocrites! For you bar the entrance into the Kingdom of God in the faces of men; for you don't enter, and you don't allow those who want to enter to go in.

Woe to you, scribes and Pharisees, hypocrites! For you devour widows' houses, and pretend to be sincere by praying a long prayer: and so you will receive greater condemnation.

Woe to you, scribes and Pharisees, hypocrites! You circle the sea and land to make one convert, and when he is made, you make him two times more a son of hell than yourselves.

Woe unto you, blind guides, who say, whoever swears by the Temple, it means nothing; but whoever shall swear by the gold of the Temple, the oath is binding. You blind fools: for which is greater, the gold, or the Temple that sanctifies the gold for God? And you say, whoever shall swear by the altar of burnt offerings, it means nothing; but whoever swears by the gift on the altar, the oath is binding. You blind fools: which is greater, the gift, or the altar that sanctifies the gift for God? Therefore, he who swears by the altar, swears by it, and by all that is on it. And whoever swears by the Temple, swears by it, and by Him that dwells in it. And he that swears by Heaven, swears by the throne of God, and by the One seated upon it.

Woe unto you, scribes and Pharisees, hypocrites! Because you're careful to tithe of garden mint, dill seed, and caraway seed, and have omitted the weightier matters of the Law such as justice, mercy, and faithfulness. These things you ought to have done, and not left the others undone. You are blind guides, who strain out a gnat, and gulp down a camel.

Woe unto you, scribes and Pharisees, hypocrites! For you clean the outside of the cup and dish, but inside they are filled with extortion and excess. You blind Pharisee, clean the inside of the cup first, so that the outside may be clean also.

Woe unto you, scribes and Pharisees, hypocrites! You are like whitewashed graves which appear beautiful on the outside, but inside are full of dead men's bones and all kinds of uncleanness. In the same way, you appear to be righteous on the outside for men to see, but inside you are full of hypocrisy and lawlessness.

Woe unto you, scribes and Pharisees, hypocrites! You build the tombs of the prophets, and adorn the monuments of the righteous, and say, 'If we had lived in the days of our fathers, we would not have been partakers with them in shedding the blood of the prophets.' Therefore you testify against yourselves that you are the children of them who killed the prophets. Fill up what is lacking of the sins of your fathers. You snakes, generation of vipers, how can you possibly escape the judgment of hell?

On account of this, I send prophets, wise men, and scribes to you: and some of them you will kill and crucify; and some of them you will scourge in your synagogues, and persecute from city to city: so that all the righteous blood that has been shed upon the earth may come upon you, from the blood of Abel, the righteous one, to the blood of Zachariah, son of Barachiah, whom you murdered between the inner sanctuary and the altar of burnt offerings. I assure you, all these things shall come upon this generation.

O Jerusalem, Jerusalem, the city that kills the prophets, and stones those who are sent to you. How often did I long to gather your children together to Myself, like a hen gathers her chicks under her wings, but you didn't want me to. Behold, your house is left to you desolate and abandoned. For I say to you, you shall not see Me from this time forward, until you say, 'Blessed is He Who comes in the name of the Lord.'

After these sayings, Jesus turned and walked away from the Jewish leaders with His disciples following, and ascended the flight of stairs that led from the Terrace into the Temple building. When they reached the top, where they had a full view of the Court of the Women, they passed through one of the gates, and Jesus sat down. He watched as people threw money into the treasury, made up of the 13 trumpet shaped containers. A line of people were tossing their coins in the various containers, and several of the wealthy put in great sums. But in the midst of the crowd stood a certain poor widow who was holding two small copper coins. The Lord called His disciples over and pointed toward the lady, and they watched as she dropped in the two mites.

He said, "Truly I say to you, this poverty stricken widow put in more than all those who threw into the Treasury: because these all tossed in out of their abundance; but she cast in all that she had for her life's necessities."

With that, Jesus made His way out of the Temple for the last time.

CHAPTER 34

As Jesus was leaving, the disciples began to comment on the beauty of the enormous stones that made up the Temple.

One said to Jesus, "Lord, do you see what kind of stones and buildings these are?"

He replied, "Do you see these great buildings? There is coming a day when not one stone you're looking at will be left on another. They will all be thrown down."

They quietly crossed the deep ravine of the Kidron Valley and began to travel up the side of the Mount of Olives. As they came around a sudden turn in the road, the entire Temple came into view. As they looked down, they could see its enclosures, colonnades, and halls, as well as the sanctuary itself. They were made up of massive stones, some from twenty to forty feet long, and six feet thick, weighing up to 100 tons. Jesus sat down and was joined by Peter, Andrew, James, and John, who wanted to talk to Him privately.

"Teacher, tell us when the things you were talking about will happen? And what shall be the sign of your coming, and the end of the world?"

Jesus answered, "See to it that no one leads you astray. Many will come in My Name, saying, 'I am Christ,' and, 'The Time is drawing near,' and deceive many. Don't go after them. And you're going to hear of wars, and rumors of wars, as well as other commotions; and when you do, don't be terrified. These things need to happen, but this is not the end. For nation shall rise against nation, and kingdom against kingdom. There shall be great earthquakes in various places, famines, pestilences, and other disturbing things, as well as great signs in the heavens. But these are only the beginning of sorrow and anguish.

But take heed to yourselves, because before all this they shall lay hands on you, and persecute you. They will deliver you to councils, and you will be beaten in the synagogues, put in prison, and some will even be killed. Then many shall be offended, and shall betray and hate one another. And many false prophets shall arise, and lead many astray; and because iniquity will multiply, the love of many will grow cold.

You shall be brought before kings and governors for My Name's sake. This will turn out to be to your advantage, since it will be a testimony of your loyalty. Decide in your hearts not to meditate beforehand how you'll defend yourself against the charges brought against you, but say whatever is given to you in that hour. You will not be the ones who are speaking, but it will be the Holy Spirit.

Brother will betray brother to death, and a father, a child, and children shall rise up against their parents and will cause them to put to death. You shall be hated by all men for My Names' sake; but he that endures to the end will be saved. Not a hair of your head will perish. And this Gospel of the Kingdom shall be preached in all the world for a testimony to all nations, and then the end will come.

When you see the abomination of desolation, which Daniel

the Prophet spoke about, standing in the Holy Place where he shouldn't be, and when you see Jerusalem being surrounded by armies, recognize that its desolation is near. Then let those who are in Judea flee to the mountains, and let him which is on the housetop not go down and enter into his house to get anything, and don't let him who is in the fields return even to get his clothes.

Woe to them that are pregnant and to those who are nursing their young in those days. And pray that your flight may not be in the winter nor on the Sabbath Day. For there will be great distress in the land, and wrath on this people; and they shall fall by the edge of the sword, and shall be led away captive into all nations. Jerusalem shall be crushed under the heel of the conquering Gentiles, until the time of their domination is over. For then there shall be great tribulation such as has not occurred from the beginning of God's creation until now, nor ever shall be again. And if the Lord had not shortened those days, no flesh would be saved from destruction. But for the sake of the elect whom God chose out, they will be shortened.

Then, if anyone says to you, 'Behold, here is Christ,' or, 'look, He's there,' don't believe them. For false Christs and false prophets will arise and will perform signs and wonders in order to deceive and lead away the very elect. Look, I've told you ahead of time. Therefore, if they say to you, 'Look, He's in the desert'; don't go out. 'Look, He's in the secret rooms'; don't even begin to believe it. For just as the lightning shines out of the east and is seen even to the west, so shall the coming of the Son of Man be; for wherever the carcass is, that's where the vultures will be gathered together.

Immediately after the tribulation of those days, there shall be signs in the sun, and in the moon, and in the stars. The sun shall be darkened, and the moon will not give her light, and the stars will be seen falling from Heaven, and the powers that control the Heavenly bodies shall be shaken. Upon the earth there will be national distress in the midst of perplexity; the sea and waves roaring, men's hearts failing because of fear and expectation of the things that are coming on the earth.

Then shall they see the sign of the Son of Man in Heaven, and then shall all the people of the earth mourn in anguish, and they shall see the Son of Man coming with the clouds of Heaven with power and great glory. And he shall send His angels with the sound of a great trumpet, and they shall gather together His elect from the four winds, from one end of the Heavens to the other. When these things begin to take place, then lift up your heads and look up, because your redemption is drawing near.

Now, learn a lesson from the fig tree. When the branch becomes tender and puts forth leaves, you understand that summer is near. Likewise, when you see all these things coming to pass, you'll know that the Kingdom of God is near, even at the door. I assure you, this race and nation shall never ever pass away until every one of these things come to pass. Heaven and earth shall pass away, but My words shall never pass away.

But concerning that day and hour no one knows, not even the angels in Heaven nor even the Son, but only the Father. Because just as the days of Noah were, so shall it be at the time of the coming of the Son man. For in the days before the flood they were eating and drinking, marrying and giving in marriage, until the day Noah entered the Ark; and they didn't know until the Flood took them away. So shall it be at the time of the coming of the Son of Man. Then there will be two in the field; one shall be taken, and the other left. Two women shall be grinding at the mill. One shall be taken, and one shall be left. Be constantly paying attention, watching and praying, for you don't know when the time will be. And take heed to yourselves, lest at any time your hearts are weighed down by drunkenness and intoxication, and the cares of this life, so that that day should burst upon you unexpectedly; for as a snare it shall come upon all those who are living on the face of all the earth."

As the Apostles listened Jesus continued.

"It is just like a man who has gone off to another country. When he left his house, he gave his servants authority as well as instructions for what he wanted them to do during his absence, and commanded the doorkeeper to be constantly alert and watching. Therefore, be constantly alert and on the watch: for you do not know when the master of the house is coming, whether at evening, or at midnight, or at cockcrowing, or in the morning; lest he comes unexpectedly and finds you slumbering.

But realize this: if the master of the house had known at what hour of the night the thief was coming, he would have been on guard, and would not have allowed his house to be broken into. Therefore you also be ready, because in an hour when you don't think it will be, the Son of Man will come. So be attentive and ready, and always praying that you may have the strength to escape all these things that are about to take place, and to stand before the Son of Man. And what I'm saying to you I say to all, 'watch.'

Who, then, is a faithful and wise servant, whom the master appointed over his household to give them their food at the proper time? Blessed is that servant, who, when his master comes, will be found doing this. I assure you that he will appoint him over all his possessions. But if that servant is evil, and should say in his heart, 'My master is delaying His coming', and shall begin to beat his fellow servants, and to eat and drink with those who are drunk, the master of that servant will come on a day when he is not expecting Him, and at an hour he doesn't know. And he shall punish him severely, and shall appoint him his portion with the hypocrites in the place where there shall be weeping and gnashing of teeth.

The Kingdom of Heaven shall be likened to ten virgins that took their lamps and went out to meet the bridegroom. Five of them were wise, and five foolish. Those who were foolish took their lamps, but didn't take any extra oil; but the wise took containers of extra oil along with their lamps. While the bridegroom delayed his coming, they all nodded off and fell asleep. At midnight there was a cry, 'Look, the bridegroom is coming. Go out to meet him.' Then all the virgins got up and each began to prepare her lamp. The foolish said to the wise, 'Quickly, give us some of your oil, because our lamps are going out.' But the wise answered, 'We can't, we don't have enough for us and you. Instead, go to the sellers and buy your own'. While they went on their way to buy some, the bridegroom came, and those who were ready went in with him to the wedding; and the door was shut. Later, the rest of the virgins came, saying, 'Lord, Lord, open up for us.' But he answered, 'I assure you, I don't know you.' So be ever on the watch, because you don't know the day nor the hour the Son of Man is coming.

The Kingdom is also like a man who was about to travel abroad. He called his own servants, and gave them the responsibility for caring for and managing his possessions. To one he gave five talents of money, to another, two talents, and then to still another, one talent, to each one according to his ability; and then he left. He that received the five talents immediately went out and traded with them, and made a profit of five more talents. And likewise the one who had received the two did the same, and made a profit of two more. But he that received one went off, dug a hole in the ground, and buried his master's money.

After a long time, the master of the servants came back to settle accounts with them. The one who had received five talents brought five more talents as well, saying, 'Master, you gave me five talents to do business with. See, I made a profit of five more talents.' His master said to him, 'Well done, good and faithful servant, you were faithful over a few things, I will make you a ruler of many. Enter into the joy of your master.'

Then the one who had received two talents came with two more, and said, 'Master, you gave me two talents. See, I made a profit of two more talents.'

His master said, 'Well done, good and faithful servant. You were faithful over a few things, so I will make you a ruler over many. Enter into the joy of your master.'

Then the one who had received the one talent came and said, 'Master, I know by experience that you are a stern, hard man, reaping where you didn't sow, and gathering where you didn't scatter. So I was afraid, and went and hid your talent in the earth. See, here is what is yours.' His master said, 'you wicked, lazy servant. Did you know that I have a habit of reaping where I didn't sow, and gathering where I didn't scatter? Then you should at least have deposited my money with the bankers, and then when I came I would have received my money back with interest.

Take the talent from him, and give it to the one who has the ten talents: for to everyone who has, more shall be given until he has an abundance; and he who does not have, even what he has shall be taken from him. Then throw this good for nothing servant into the darkness outside, where there is weeping and gnashing of teeth.'

Now when the Son of Man comes in His glory, and all the holy angels with Him, then He will sit on His glorious throne.

And all the nations shall be gathered before Him, and He shall separate each one from another, like a shepherd separates the sheep from the goats. He shall have the sheep line up on His right hand, and the goats on the left.

The King shall say to those lined up on His right hand, 'Come, you who are blessed by My Father, and inherit the Kingdom which has been prepared for you from the foundation of the world. For I was hungry, and you gave me something to eat; I was thirsty, and you gave me a drink; I was a stranger, and you took me into your home; naked, and you clothed me. I was sick, and you looked after me; and when I was in prison, you came to see me.'

Then the righteous will answer Him, 'Lord, when did we see you hungry, and feed you; or thirsty, and give you a drink? And when did we see you a stranger, and take you in; or naked, and clothe you? Or when did we see you sick, or in prison, and come to you?' And the King will answer them, 'I assure you, in so far as you did this even to the least of My brethren, you did it to me.'

Then He shall say to those who are lined up on His left hand, 'Leave Me, you who are doomed and cursed, into the everlasting fire, which is ready for the devil and his angels. For I was hungry, and you gave Me no food; I was thirsty, and you didn't give me anything to drink.

I was a stranger, and you didn't take Me in; naked, and you didn't clothe me; sick, and in prison, and you didn't visit me.'

Then they will answer Him, 'Lord, when did we see you hungry, or thirsty, or a stranger, or naked, or sick, or in prison, and not help you?' Then He will answer, 'I assure you, in so far as you didn't do it to one of the least of people, you didn't do it to Me.' And these shall go off into everlasting punishment; but the righteous ones into eternal life."

CHAPTER 35

When Jesus had finished answering their questions, as they prepared to leave for Bethany, He said, "You know that two days from now is the Passover, and the Son of Man is going to be betrayed and crucified."

*   *   *

The chief priests, Scribes, and elders from the Sanhedrin gathered in the courtyard of the High Priest, Caiaphas. They had been in search for a while how they might use craftiness to capture Jesus and get rid of Him, but had been unsuccessful.

The only decision they agreed on was, "We can't do it during the feast because that might lead to an uproar among the people."

*   *   *

Later on that night Simon the Leper, who had been healed by Jesus, held a dinner. Lazarus, who had also been invited, sat at the table, and Martha, as usual, was serving. As the meal continued, Mary entered carrying an alabaster container of Nard, which was very fragrant and expensive. (It came from the hills of India around the banks of the Ganges River). She came up behind the Lord, and, to everyone's surprise, broke open the container and began to pour the ointment on the head of Jesus, and then on His feet. Many sitting around the table began to get upset as they saw what she was doing.

Judas Iscariot said, "This ointment could have been sold for a year's wages, and the money given to the poor. This is such a waste."

Jesus said, "Leave her alone. Why are you bothering her? She has done a beautiful thing for Me. For you have the poor with you always, and whenever you want you can do them good; but you won't always have Me. She has done what she could. She has come beforehand to anoint My body for burial. I assure you, wherever the Gospel may be proclaimed throughout the whole world, what she has done today shall be spoken of as a memorial to her."

That night the chief priests received unexpected assistance when Judas Iscariot, one of Jesus' twelve Apostles, asked to see them. He had left the home of Simon the Leper after he had been stung by the public rebuke of Jesus, and decided to get revenge for the embarrassment. He was led into where the priests and the captains of the Temple guards were eagerly waiting.

They were overjoyed when he asked, "How much are you willing to give me to hand Jesus of Nazareth over to you?"

They finally agreed to the amount of 30 pieces of silver, counted out the money, and handed it over to him. From that time on, he sought for an opportunity when there was no one around, so that he could betray Him.

*　　　*　　　*

Jesus spent the following day with His Apostles and friends, as they waited for the next day when they would gather for the Passover meal.

*　　　*　　　*

The morning of the day when the Passover lambs would be killed arrived. Jesus' disciples asked, "Where do you want us to go and prepare so that you may eat the Passover?"

He told Peter and John, "Go into Jerusalem. When you get there, you will be met by a man carrying a pot of water. Follow him wherever he goes, and when he arrives at his destination, say to the master of the house, 'The Master says, My time is near. I will keep the Passover with My disciples at your home. Where is the guest chamber that we can use?' He will show you to a large upper room, furnished and prepared. Prepare for the meal there."

So the disciples went out to the city and found everything as He said, and the upper room ready as well. They only needed to go to get the Paschal Lamb. So early that afternoon, they made their way up the Temple Mount, along with the rest of the crowd of joyous pilgrims. The Temple courts were filled to capacity with worshippers from all over Israel, and other countries as well. Thousands of priests from all 24 courses were on duty and serving the huge crowd.

They entered the Court of the Priests and the massive Nicanor gates, which led from the Court of the Women to the Court of Israel, as the other side gates were closed. At the sound of the three- fold blasts from the Priest's trumpet, each Israelite would slay his lamb, with the blood being caught in the golden bowl by the presiding priest, who handed it to another, and received an empty bowl in return. It was eventually passed on to the great altar, where it was poured out at the base. The lamb was then flayed, cleansed, and the parts which were to be burnt on the Altar removed and prepared for burning. Finally, Peter and John made their way back to the Upper Room, carrying what was left of the sacrifice.

Later that afternoon as the sun was setting, Jesus and the other Ten Apostles descended from the Mount of Olives into the Holy City. After walking through the crowded streets, they arrived at the place. They ascended to the upper room, which Peter and John had prepared. As they approached the low horseshoe shaped table, they almost immediately began to argue about where each of them should sit. The most important seat at the very center would, of course, be occupied by Jesus, but where everyone else would sit was the question. They especially contended over who should sit on either side of the Lord, since these were considered the most important seats.

Jesus said, "The kings of the Gentiles exercise lordship over them, and those who exercise authority are called benefactors. But it will not be like that with you. He who is greatest among you, let him be as the younger one; and he who is a leader, let him be as one who serves. For who is greater, the one who sits at the dinner table, or the one who serves? Isn't it the one who sits at the table? But I am in your midst as One Who serves."

When they then sat down, the Lord said, "With an intense desire I have looked forward to eating this Passover with you before I suffer; for I say to you, I will not eat of it anymore, until the time when it is fulfilled in the Kingdom of God. You are the ones who have remained with Me through My trials and tests. I am appointing to you a kingdom, just as My Father has appointed one for Me, so that you may eat and drink at My table in My Kingdom; and you shall be on thrones, judging the 12 tribes of Israel."

As the evening went on, Jesus suddenly rose to His feet. The others watched curiously as He laid aside His outer garments, took a towel, and wrapped it around Himself. Next, He poured water into a basin; and as the Apostles looked on in silent astonishment, Jesus approached Peter,and knelt down to wash his feet.

Peter asked, "Are you going to wash my feet?"

Jesus answered, "What I'm doing you don't completely understand just now, but you shall learn afterwards."

"You will never, ever, wash my feet."

"If I don't wash your feet, you have no part with Me."

"Well then, not only my feet, but my hands and head also."

"He who has been bathed all over, only has to wash his feet. All of you are clean: well, almost all of you."

He went from one man to the next washing their feet, and drying them with the towel wrapped around His waist. He finally finished, picked up His outer garments, and sat down again.

He asked, "Do you understand the meaning of what I just did? You address Me as Teacher and Lord, and you're right to do that, because that's Who I am. So then if I, your Lord and Teacher, washed your feet, you also ought to wash each other's feet; for I have given you an example that you should do as I have done. I assure you, a servant is not greater than his Master, nor an Apostle greater than the One Who sent him. Since you know these things, you are blessed if you make a habit of doing them. I'm not speaking about all of you. I know whom I have selected as an Apostle, but the Scripture must be fulfilled that says, 'He who eats bread with Me, lifted up his heel to trip Me.' From now on, I am telling you before it comes to pass, so that when it does happen, you might believe that I am He. I assure you, he who receives whoever I send, receives Me. And he who receives Me, receives Him Who sent Me."

Jesus, then, stunned everyone at the Table when He said, "I assure you, one of you shall betray Me."

The disciples began to grieve as one after another said, "Surely, it's not me."

Then Jesus added, "The Son of Man goes as it is written concerning Him, but woe to that man who betrays Him. It would be better for that man if he had never been born."

While the Apostles kept looking back and forth at each other trying to figure out whom Jesus meant, Peter motioned to John, who was leaning on Jesus' bosom, and quietly said, "Ask Jesus who it is?"

He leaned over even more closely, and asked the Lord, "Who is it?"

He answered, "It's the one whom I give the morsel to that I first dip."

Then after dipping the morsel, He gave it to Judas Iscariot. After he reached out and took the morsel, satan entered him.

Iscariot then said as all the others had, "Surely, I'm not the one, Lord."

Jesus simply looked at him, and said, "What you are doing, do even more quickly."

Judas stepped out of the room and into the night. None of the others thought anything of it, and assumed he was going to give money to the poor, or to pay for something that had to do with the Passover.

Jesus then said, "Now is the Son of Man glorified, and God is glorified in Him. If God is glorified in Him, God will also glorify Him in Himself quickly. Little children, I will be with you a little longer. You will seek Me; but just as I said to the Jews, I now say to you. Where I'm going, you cannot come. I am giving you a new commandment, that you should love one another. By this shall all men know that you are My disciples, if you have love for one another."

Simon Peter asked, "Lord, where are you going?"

"Where I'm going you can't follow Me now, but you will follow me later. Tonight, all of you shall fall away because of Me; for it's written, 'I will cut down the shepherd, and the sheep shall be scattered.' But after I am risen, I will go before you into Galilee."

But Peter said, "Even if all these men fall away, I never will."

"Simon, Simon, look: satan has desired to shake and to sift

you like wheat, to try to overthrow your faith. But I have prayed for you, that your faith doesn't fail; and when your faith is fully restored, strengthen your brothers."

"Lord, I'm ready to go with you both to prison and even to death."

"Would you lay down your life for Me? Before the rooster crows twice tonight, you'll deny you even know Me three times."

Peter repeated even more vehemently, "If I should have to die with you, I will positively never deny you."

All the others joined in, saying the same thing.

Near the end of the meal Christ took the cup of wine mixed with water, and gave thanks, saying, "Blessed art thou, Jehovah our God, King of the universe, Who has created the fruit of the vine."

He then passed it out, and said, "Take this and share it among you. Drink from it, all of you: for this is My blood of the New Testament, which is poured out for many so that sin will be put away. I will not drink anymore from the fruit of the vine until the day when I drink it new with you in the Kingdom of God."

After they had all drunk of the cup, Jesus took the piece of unleavened bread, which had been set aside at the beginning of the meal.

He pronounced the blessing, "Blessed art Thou, Jehovah our God, King of the Universe, Who has brought forth bread from the earth."

He then broke it, gave it to them, and said, "Take this and eat it; for this is My body, which is given for You. Always do this in remembrance of Me."

CHAPTER 36

Jesus knew that much of what He had said during the evening had been upsetting to His Apostles.

He said, "Don't let your heart be troubled. Believe in God, and believe also in Me. In My Father's house are many mansions. If that were not so, I would have told you; for I go to prepare a place for you. And if I go to prepare a place for you, I will come again and receive you to myself, so that where I am you may be also. You know where I'm going, and you know the way."

Thomas responded, "Lord, we don't know where you are going, so how can we possibly know the way?"

Jesus answered, "I alone am the Way, the Truth, and the Life. No one comes to the Father, except by Me. If you had known Me, you should have come to know My Father also. From now on you are beginning to know Him, and you have seen Him."

Philip said, "Lord, show us the Father, and that will be enough for us."

He answered, "Have I been with you this long, and yet you haven't known Me, Philip? He who has seen Me has seen the Father. So how can you say, 'Show us the Father?' Don't you believe that I am in the Father and that the Father is in Me? I am not the source of the words which I am speaking to you. But the Father Who dwells in Me is doing His work. Believe Me that I am in the Father and that the Father is in Me. But if not, believe on account of the works themselves that you've seen. I assure you, he that believes in Me, that person shall do the works that I do, and even greater works, because I go unto My Father. And whatever you ask in My Name, I will do so, that the Father may be glorified in the Son. If you ask anything in My Name, I'll do it. If you love me, you will keep My commandments.

I will ask the Father, and He will give you another Comforter like Me, so that He might be with you forever. He is the Spirit of Truth; Whom the world can't receive, because it doesn't see Him, nor know Him. But you know Him; for He dwells by your side, and shall be in you. I will not leave you behind helpless, but I will come to you. Yet a little while and the world will no longer see Me; but you will see Me. Because I live, you shall live also. In that day you shall know that I am in My Father, and you in me, and I in You.

He who has My commandments and keeps them is the one who loves Me. And he who loves Me will be loved by My Father, and I will love him, and will reveal Myself to Him."

The other Judas said, "Lord, what has happened that made it so you will reveal yourself to us, but not to the world?"

Jesus answered, "If anyone loves Me, he will keep My words; and My Father will love him, and we will come to him, and we'll make our home with him. These things I have spoken to you while I'm still with you. But the Comforter, Who is the Holy Spirit, Whom the Father will send in My Name, He will teach you all things, and remind you of all the things I have spoken to you.

I leave peace with you, and it is My peace I give to you. I don't give you what the world gives. Don't let your heart be troubled, neither let it be afraid. You have heard that I said to you, I am leaving, and I will return to you. If you loved Me, you would already have rejoiced, because I have said that I am going to the Father: for My Father is greater than I. And now I have told you before it happens, so that when it does, you might believe. I will not speak many things with you, for the ruler of this world comes, and He has nothing in Me. I do as My Father has commanded Me, so that the world may know that I love the Father. Arise, let's go."

*   *   *

With that, Jesus and His remaining 11 Apostles descended from the Upper Room into the street. They began to make their way to a place Jesus went often to pray- the Garden of Gethsemane. It was a place Judas Iscariot knew well also. As they walked, they stopped by one of the many vineyards that were literally all over Israel. Almost every village in the hill country was surrounded by vineyards, and had at least one winepress for processing the grape harvest. As they stood looking, Jesus began to teach them.

"I am the only genuine vine, and My Father is the One Who tills the soil. Every branch in Me that doesn't bear fruit, He takes away. And every branch that bears fruit, He prunes and cleanses so that it keeps on bearing and perhaps produces even more fruit. Now you are cleansed because of the Word I have spoken to you.

Abide in Me, and I will abide with you. Just as a branch cannot bear fruit from itself unless it remains united to the vine, neither can you bear fruit unless you have a living union with Me. I am the Vine, you are the branches: He that maintains a living union with Me, and I with Him, bears much fruit: because apart from Me you can do nothing.

If a person does not have a living union with Me, he is cast aside as a branch would be, and withers. They are then gathered together, thrown into the fire, and burned. If you maintain that living union with Me, and My words are at home in you, ask what your heart desires, and it will be yours. My Father is glorified by you bearing much fruit, and so shall you be My disciples.

Just as the Father loved Me, I also have loved you. Remain in My love. If you keep My commandments, you remain in My love; just as I have kept My Father's commandments, and remain in His love. I have spoken these things to you so that My joy might be in you, and that your joy might be filled to the fullest.

This is My commandment, that you love one another, just as I love you. Greater love has no one than this, that someone lays down his life for his friends. You are My friends, if you make a habit of doing whatever I command you. I no longer call you servants, because the servant doesn't know what his master is doing. But you have I called friends, because I have made known to you all that I heard from My Father. You have not chosen Me, but I have chosen you for Myself, and appointed you to go forth and bear fruit, and that your fruit should remain. This is so that whatever you shall ask the Father in My Name, He may give it to you. These things I command you, that you love one another.

If the world hates you, you know that it hated Me, and, in fact, still does, before it hated you. If you were of the world, in that case the world would love what is its own. But because you are not of this world, but I have chosen you out of this world for Myself, so the world hates you. Remember the word that I spoke to you, a servant is not greater than his master. Since they persecuted Me, you will be persecuted too. If they kept My Word, they will keep yours also. But all these things they will do to you on account of My Name, because they don't know the One who sent me.

If I had not come and spoken unto them, they would not have had sin. But now they have no way to conceal their sin. He that hates Me, hates My Father also. If I had not done among them works that no one else had ever done, they would not have sin. But now they have seen and hated Me and My Father, and continue to do so. But this has come to pass so that the word that is written in their Law might be fulfilled, 'They hated Me for no reason.'

When the Comforter comes, Whom I will send to you from My Father, even the Spirit of Truth, Who proceeds from My Father's presence, He will testify of Me. And you also shall bear testimony, because you have been with Me from the beginning."

Jesus went on teaching as they continued toward the city gates.

"I have spoken these things to you, so that you will not be made to stumble. They will put you out of the synagogues. In fact, the time is coming that everyone who kills you will think that they are doing a sacred service for God. And they'll do these things to you, because they don't know the Father, nor Me.

But now I am going away to Him Who sent Me, and yet not one of you is asking Me, 'Where are you going?' But because I have said all these things to you, sorrow has filled your hearts. But I'm telling you the truth. It is better for you that I go away. For if I don't go away, the Comforter will positively not come to you. But if I go, I will send Him to you. And when He comes, He will convict the world of sin, of righteousness, and of judgment. Of sin, because they don't believe in Me; of righteousness, because I go back to My Father, and they no longer see Me; and of judgment, because the ruler of this world stands condemned.

I still have many things to say to you, but you're not able to receive and understand them now. However, when He, the Spirit of Truth, comes, He will guide you into all truth: for He will not speak from Himself as a source; but whatever he hears is what He will speak: and he will make known to you the things that are coming. He shall glorify Me: for He shall take from that which is Mine, and make it known to you. All things that the Father has are Mine. On account of this I said, that He takes that which is Mine, and shall make it known to you. In a little while, you will no longer see Me: and again, a little while, and you will see me, because I go to the Father."

Some of His disciples said to one another, "What is this that He is saying to us, 'in a little while, and you shall not see Me,' and, 'again, in a little while, and you shall see Me,' and, 'because I'm going away to My Father?' What is this that He is saying, 'a little while?' We don't know what He is talking about."

Jesus knew that they wanted to ask Him, and so He said, "Are you inquiring among yourselves what I meant by, 'in a little while, and you shall not see Me,' and, 'again, in a little while, and you shall see me?' I assure you, you shall weep and mourn, but the world shall rejoice. You shall be made sorrowful, but your sorrow shall be turned to joy. When a woman is about to give birth she has sorrow and grief, because her hour has come. But when she bears the child, she no longer remembers her anguish, because of the joy that a man was born into the world. You now will have sorrow and grief: but I will see you again, and your heart will rejoice, and no one will take your joy away from you.

In that day, you shall not question Me about anything. I assure you, whatever you shall ask the Father in My Name, He will give it to you. Up till now you have not asked for even one thing in My Name. Continuously ask, and you shall receive, so that your joy might be completely fulfilled. These things I have spoken to you in proverbs and illustrations. But the time is coming when I will no longer speak to you that way, but I will tell you plainly about the Father.

In that day you shall ask something for yourself in My Name: and I don't say to you that I will ask the Father on your behalf: for the Father Himself loves you, because you love Me, and believe that I came from God. I came out from the Father, and have come into the world. Again, I leave the world behind, and go to the Father."

His disciples said, "Behold, now you're speaking plainly, and expressing your thoughts without a proverb. Now we know positively that you know all things, and you don't need anyone to question you. By this we believe that you came from God."

He answered, "Do you believe now? See, the hour is coming, and, as a matter of fact, has now arrived, that you will be scattered, every man to his own home, and you will leave Me alone. Yet I am not really alone, because the Father is with Me. I have spoken these things to you, that in Me you might have peace. In the world you will have tribulation: but have courage; for I have overcome the world."

CHAPTER 37

As they passed out by the gate north of the Temple, they descended to a lonely part of the darkened Kidron River Valley. Jesus stopped, lifted His eyes to Heaven, and began to talk to His Father.

"Father, the hour has come. Glorify Your Son, so that the Son may glorify You: as You gave Him authority over all flesh, so that He should give eternal life to all you have given Him. And this is eternal life, namely, that they might know You the only true God, and Jesus Christ, Whom You have sent.

I glorified you on the earth by completing what you gave Me to do. And now, O Father, glorify Me with Yourself with the glory I had with You before the world even existed. I made known Your Name to the men whom You gave Me as a gift, and they have held firmly to Your Word. Now they have come to know that all things, as many as have been given to Me, are from You. For I have given them the words You gave Me; and they have received them, and truly recognized that I came from you, and they believe that you sent Me.

Right now, I make request concerning them. I don't make request for the world, but for those you have given Me; because they are yours. And all things that are mine are yours, and the things that are yours are mine; and I am glorified in them. And now I am no longer in the world, but they remain in the world, and I come to you. O Holy Father, keep through Your own name those whom You have given Me, so that they may be one, just as We are one. While I was in the world, I was the One Who watched carefully over them in Your Name: and I guarded the ones you gave Me, and not one of them was lost, except the son of perdition; so that the Scriptures might be fulfilled.

And now I come to you; and I speak these things in the world, that they might have My joy completely fulfilled in themselves. I have given them your Word; and the world hated them, because they are not of the world, even as I am not of the world. I don't ask that you should take them out of the world, but that you should guard them and keep them safely out of the reach of the evil one. They are not of the world, even as I am not of the world. Sanctify them in Your Word, which is truth. As You sent Me into the world, so I sent them into the world. And I sanctify and set Myself apart for their sakes, so that they also might be continually sanctified in the truth.

And I don't make request only for these men, but also for those who will believe in Me through their words; so that they all might be one; even as You, Father, are in Me, and I in You, so that they also might be one in Us: and that the world may believe that You sent Me. And the glory you gave Me I have given them; so that they might be one, even as We are one: I in them, and You in Me, in order that they may be complete in oneness; and that the world might understand that you sent Me, and that you love them, even as You loved Me.

Father, I desire that they also, whom You have given Me, may be where I am; so that they might see My glory, which You gave to Me: because You loved Me before the foundation of the world. O Righteous Father, the world has not known You: yet I have known You, and these men know that You sent Me. And I have made Your Name known to them, and will continue to make it known: so that the love with which You love Me might be in them, and I might be in them."

With that, Jesus finished His prayer and they resumed their journey crossing over the Kidron River. After passing over it, they turned towards the left and picked up the road that led to the Mount of Olives. After going a few more steps, they turned to the right, until they arrived at their destination- The Garden of Gethsemane, which was on the lower western slope of the Mount of Olives, near the Judean wilderness.

As they entered the Garden, the eleven men who accompanied Jesus had no idea of the danger that was approaching, but, of course, Christ did. He said to His Apostles, "Sit here while I go and pray over there. You should pray, too, so that you don't enter into temptation."

He took Peter, James, and John with Him, leaving the other eight waiting at the entrance. With each step that He took further into the Garden, the more sorrowful and distressed He became. He began to become alarmed, and said to the three with Him, "My soul is overwhelmed with grief, so that I could almost die. Stay here and watch with Me."

He withdrew a stone's throw away, fell on His knees, and began to pray, "Father, if You are willing, remove this cup from Me. Nevertheless let not My will, but Yours, be done."

An angel from Heaven appeared to Him to strengthen Him. Entering into a state of agony, He prayed even more earnestly, and His sweat became like great drops of blood falling down upon the ground.

He fell on His face, and said, "Abba, Father, all things are possible to You. Take this cup away from Me. But not what I desire, but what You desire be done."

He got up and went to His Apostles, and found them dropping off to sleep.

He said to Peter, "Simon, are you sleeping? Didn't you have the strength to watch with Me for an hour? Watch and pray, so that you don't enter into temptation. The spirit is indeed willing, but the flesh is weak."

He went away again a second time, and prayed, "O My Father, if it is not possible that this cup pass unless I drink it, let your will be done."

And when He rose again from praying, He came to His disciples and found them fast asleep; for their eyes were heavy from sorrow.

He said, "Why are you sleeping? Rise and pray, so that you don't enter into temptation."

They didn't know what to say to Him. He went away again the third time and prayed the same words again.

He came back a third time, and said, "Sleep on now, and get your rest."

Finally he announced, "That's enough. The hour has come. Behold, the Son of Man is being betrayed into the hands of sinners. Get up. Let's be going. Look, My betrayer is here."

As He spoke, Judas, one of the twelve, with a large crowd holding lanterns and torches, and armed with swords and clubs, approached the garden. They had been sent by the chief priests and the Sanhedrin. Judas had given them a sign, so that they would know who they were to arrest. That sign was a kiss. As Judas and the mob entered the garden, Jesus and the three Apostles with Him joined the other eight.

Judas left the crowd waiting, approached Jesus, and said, "Rabbi, Rabbi."

Jesus asked, "Friend, why are you here?"

Judas embraced Him, and tenderly kissed Him.

Jesus asked, "Judas, do you betray the Son of Man with a kiss?"

Before the crowd could respond, Jesus went out to them and asked, "Who are you looking for?"

As Judas stood with them, they answered, "Jesus of

Nazareth."

He admitted to them, "I Am."

As soon as He said those words, they fell backward onto the ground. He repeated His question.

"Who are you looking for?"

They answered, "Jesus, the one from Nazareth."

He said, "I told you that that's Who I am. So since I'm the one you're looking for, let these other men go."

When the disciples around Him saw what was about to happen, they asked, "Lord, should we strike them with the sword?"

Before the question could be answered, Peter drew out one of the swords they had brought and struck a servant of the High Priest, named Malchus, and cut off his right ear.

Jesus said to Peter, "Put your sword away: for all that take the sword shall perish with the sword. Do you think I can't call on My Father, and He will provide Me this very moment with more than twelve legions of angels? Shall I not drink the cup which My Father has given Me?"

Then Jesus touched the ear of Malchus, and healed him. He turned His attention to the crowd, and asked, "Did you come out as against a robber, with swords and clubs? I was with you every day in the Temple, and you didn't stretch out your hand against Me. But this is your hour, and the power of darkness."

The soldiers, their captain, and the officers of the Jews who had accompanied the mob, arrested and bound Jesus. Then all the Apostles deserted Him, and fled. And another follower of Jesus, who had thrown a linen cloth around his nakedness and had come to the Garden, was also seized; but he fled from them naked, leaving the linen cloth behind.

*   *   *

They led the Lord back through the same gate that He and His Apostles had departed from earlier, and went up to the

Palace of Annas, located on the slope between the Upper City and the Tyropaenon. He was the father in law of Caiaphas, who was the High Priest that year. From there, Annas sent Him bound to the High Priest. Peter followed from a distance, along with John, to see what would happen. John knew the High Priest, and was allowed into the palace. Peter waited outside while John spoke to the doorkeeper, who then allowed him to enter.

As he passed her, she asked Peter, "You're not one of this Man's disciples, are you?"

He replied, "No, I'm not."

It was a cold night, and the officers and servants were sitting by a fire that had been started in the middle of the courtyard, and so Peter joined them.

Inside, Jesus was brought before Caiaphas, who questioned Him about His disciples and His teaching.

He answered, "I spoke openly to the world; I always taught in the synagogues, and in the Temple, where all the Jews come together; and said nothing in secret. Why are you asking Me? Ask those who heard Me. They know what I said."

One of the officers who was standing by slapped Jesus in the face, and said, "Is that the way you speak to the High Priest?"

Jesus demanded, "If I have said something wrong, prove it. Bear witness to the evil. But if I have spoken well, why did you hit Me?"

As all this was happening, the chief priests, elders, and scribes were gathering together. Peter was sitting in the courtyard below the palace with the guards, when one of the servants of the High Priest saw him warming himself. She said to him, "You were with Jesus from Nazareth in Galilee."

Peter replied, "I don't know what you are talking about. I don't know the man."

The chief priests and the entire Sanhedrin were seeking witnesses against Jesus, but were unsuccessful. Although there were several people who stepped up to bear false witness against Him, their testimonies didn't agree with one another. The last two witnesses stepped up.

One said, "We heard Him say, 'I will destroy this temple which is made with hands, and within three days I will build another made without hands.'"

The other said, "This fellow said, 'I am able to destroy the Temple of God, and to build it in three days.'"

Their testimonies didn't harmonize either.

The High Priest stood up in the middle of the council, and asked Jesus, "Aren't you going to answer even one thing? What are these testifying against you?"

Jesus remained silent.

Finally Caiaphas said to Him, "I place you under oath by the living God, that you tell us whether you are the Christ, the Son of God."

Jesus said, "I Am. More than that, you will see the Son of Man sitting on the right hand of Power, and coming with the clouds of Heaven."

The High Priest tore his outer robes, and cried out, "Now you've heard Him! Why do we still need witnesses? What do you think?"

They all answered, "He is guilty of death!"

The men that held Jesus began to mock and beat Him. Certain ones began to spit on Him.

They then blindfolded Him, and began to punch Him, and challenged Him, saying, "Prophesy, Who struck you?"

The officers slapped Him across the face, and they spoke many blasphemous things against Him.

An hour had passed by when some who stood by approached Peter.

They said, "You surely were with Him, for you are a Galilean. The way you speak gives you away."

Then one of the High Priest's servants, who was a relative of the one whose ear Peter cut off, asked, "Didn't I see you in the garden with Him?"

Peter began to curse and swear, and said, "I don't know who you're talking about."

At that moment, Peter was startled by the sound of a rooster crowing; and when he looked up, he saw Jesus looking at Him. He remembered how the Lord had told him that before the rooster crowed, he would deny he knew Jesus three times. Peter burst into tears, and rushed out weeping bitterly.

CHAPTER 38

At dawn the next morning, all the chief priests, scribes, and elders of the people, along with the entire Sanhedrin, met in a council together to put Jesus to death. He was led in, and the questioning began once more.

"If you are the Christ, tell us!"

He said to them, "If I tell you, you would never believe. And if I put a question to you, you never answer Me. But from this time forth, the Son of Man shall be seated on the right hand of the power of God."

They all said, "So, you are the Son of God."

He answered, "It is as you say."

They concluded, "Why do we need other witnesses? We ourselves have heard it from His Own mouth."

So they bound Him and led Him away to Pontius Pilate, the governor.

When Judas saw that Jesus had been condemned, he regretted what he had done. He entered the Temple courtyard through the Huldah gate in search of the priests and elders. When he finally found them, he approached them and said, "I have sinned, and betrayed innocent blood."

They simply said, "What is that to us? You see to it."

As they turned away and went on speaking, Judas rushed forward, and with all his might hurled the pieces of silver towards the Sanctuary itself. Then he went off and hanged himself.

The chief priests gathered the coins from off the floor. They said, "It's not legal to put the money into the sacred treasury, since it's the price of blood."

After consulting with one another, they used the money to buy the ground where the potters dug their clay, to be used as a place to bury strangers, which they called, 'The Field of Blood.'

*   *   *

The whole multitude of the Jewish elders and priests led Jesus to Pilate's official residence. They didn't want to enter the palace, because they would be defiled and not able to eat the Passover, so Pilate came out to them.

"What formal accusation are you bringing against this man?"

They answered, "If this man wasn't an evildoer, we wouldn't have delivered Him up to you."

Then Pilate said, "You take Him yourselves and judge Him according to your Law."

The Jews replied, "It's not legal for us to put anyone to death."

Then they began to accuse Him.

"We investigated this Man and found Him corrupting our nation, forbidding us to pay taxes to Caesar, and saying that He is Christ, a King."

So Pilate asked Jesus, "Are you the King of the Jews?"

Jesus said, "It's as you say."

The accusations resumed as the chief priests added more

and more charges, but Jesus didn't say a word.

Pilate asked, "Aren't you going to answer these charges? Don't you hear all these things that they bear witness against you?"

But Jesus still didn't say a word, and Pilate was amazed. Finally the governor ordered Jesus to accompany him back into the judgment hall.

Pilate asked, "Are you the King of the Jews?"

Jesus answered, "Are you yourself saying this, or did others say this about me?"

"I'm not a Jew, am I? Your own nation and chief priests delivered you over to me. What did you do?"

"My Kingdom is not of this world. If My kingdom were of this world, then My servants would be fighting right now, to keep Me from being delivered to the Jews. But My kingdom is not from here."

"So, you are a king?"

"You say that I am a King. I have been born and have come into this world for a purpose- that I should bear witness of the truth. Everyone who is of the truth hears My voice."

Pilate replied, "What is truth?"

He went back out to the chief priests and the crowds that had gathered, and announced, "I don't find this man responsible for one solitary wrong thing."

They grew even angrier.

"He is always trying to stir up the Jewish nation, from when he began in Galilee, and right up till now."

When Pilate heard them say, 'Galilee,' he saw an opportunity to be rescued from this situation. He asked whether the man was a Galilean. As soon as he found out that Jesus belonged to Herod's jurisdiction, he sent Him away to Herod, who was also in Jerusalem at that time.

*   *   *

The chief priests and Scribes led Jesus to the old Maccabean Palace where Herod Antipas was staying. It had been built decades earlier by Jewish kings of the Hasmonean dynasty, who ruled the Promised Land as an independent state before the Romans came.

When Herod saw Jesus, he was thrilled because he had heard about many of the things He had done, and for a long time he had hoped to witness Him perform a miracle. Now he would possibly have his chance, but instead, as he asked the Lord question after question, He stood in silence. The Jewish leaders who had been standing by began to vehemently accuse Him. As Herod realized that Jesus was not going to cooperate, he and his soldiers began to mock Him, as well and treat Him as nothing. Finally, they insultingly threw a brilliant robe around Him and sent Him back to Pilate.

*   *   *

When Jesus was brought back to the Praetorium, Pilate called the chief priests, rulers, and common people together. He said, "You have brought this man to me as one who stirs up the people, and I have examined Him here in front of you. I haven't found Him guilty of a single thing you are accusing him of. King Herod didn't find any reason to put Him to death either and instead sent Him back here. So, I'm going to scourge Him and let Him go."

Each year the governor had a custom of releasing a prisoner that the crowd would want. The people began to ask him to do the same thing this year. They had a notorious prisoner named Barabbas, who had been thrown into prison for leading a rebellion among the people, as well as for robbery and murder.

Pilate asked, "Who do you want me to release to you? Barabbas, or Jesus Who is called Christ?"

He asked this because he was beginning to realize that the religious leaders had delivered Jesus to him because of envy. As he sat on the judgment seat, waiting for their answer, his wife sent him a message.

"Don't have anything to do with what happens to that just man; for I have suffered many things today in a dream because of Him."

The chief priest and elders stirred up the crowd and persuaded them to call for the release of Barabbas, and for Jesus to be destroyed.

So when he asked who they wanted to have released, they said, "Barabbas."

Pilate then asked, "What will I do with Him Whom you call King of the Jews?"

They cried out, "Crucify Him."

Pilate, who wanted to release Christ, spoke to them again.

"Why? What evil did this man do? I haven't found one cause of death in Him; so I'll scourge Him, and then release Him."

He was taken away to a place where He was bound to a low stake, and scourged with leather thongs, tipped with lead balls and sharp spikes. He was beaten mercilessly until His body was covered by gouges and wounds that looked like bloody stripes. Afterwards he was taken to the Common Hall, where the whole detachment of soldiers gathered around Him. They stripped Him of His bloodstained clothes, threw a faded scarlet robe that looked like purple around Him, and took a crown of thorns they had woven and pressed it down into His head.

They put a staff made out of a reed into His right hand, and began to fall on their knees in mock reverence, saying, "Hail, King of the Jews." They spat on Him repeatedly, and kept on beating Him over the head with the reed, and slapping Him.

*   *   *

Sometime later, Pilate came outside again, and said, "Look! I'm bringing Him out to you so that you may know that I don't find any cause to accuse Him."

Jesus came out wearing the purple robe and crown of thorns. Pilate said, "Behold the Man!"

When the chief priests and officers caught sight of Him, they cried out, "Crucify Him, crucify Him!"

The governor responded, "You take Him and crucify Him; for I find no fault in Him."

The Jews answered, "Whatever you may say, we have a law; and according to that law He should die, because He made Himself the Son of God."

When Pilate heard that, he was even more afraid, and took Jesus back into the palace again.

He asked Jesus, "Where do you come from?"

Christ stood silently.

Pilate said, "You refuse to speak to me? Don't you realize that I have the authority to crucify you, and the authority to release you?"

Jesus answered, "You wouldn't have any authority over Me, except that it has been given to you from above. Because of this, the one who handed Me over to you has the greater sin."

This caused Pilate to renew his efforts to release Him, but the Jews said, "If you release this fellow, you are no friend of Caesar. Whoever makes himself a king, as this man has, declares that He is against Caesar."

When Pilate heard these words, he brought Jesus out, and sat down in the judgment seat in a place called "the Pavement." It was now about six in the morning of the preparation day for the Passover.

Pilate said, "Behold your King."

They cried out, "Take Him away! Take Him away! Crucify Him!"

He asked, "Shall I crucify your King?"

The chief priests answered, "We have no king but Caesar."

Pilate saw that he was accomplishing nothing, but causing an uproar. He called for water to be brought out, and washed his hands in the sight of the crowd.

He said, "I am innocent of the blood of this just man. You see to it."

All the people answered, "Let His blood be upon us, and on our children."

He released Barabbas, and handed Christ over to them, and they led Him away to be crucified.

CHAPTER 39

A centurion led the way up the Via Dolorosa, followed by Jesus of Nazareth Who was burdened down by His cross. The purple robe had been torn from His battered body, and replaced again by His own bloody robe. He was surrounded by four soldiers, as were the other two condemned criminals following closely behind. As they continued up the steep trek to Golgotha, Jesus fell under the weight of His Cross. The soldiers seized a Cyrenian named Simon, who was coming from the farming district, and forced him to carry His cross, following after Jesus.   A large crowd of people gathered along the route, including women who were beating their breasts out of grief, and lamenting Him. Jesus suddenly stopped, turned around, and faced those following.

"Daughters of Jerusalem, don't weep for Me, but for yourselves, and for your children. For, behold, the days are coming when they will say, 'blessed are those who have never given birth, and the wombs that have never borne, and the breasts which have never given nourishment.' Then they will begin to say to the mountains, 'fall on us!' and to the hills, 'Cover us!' For if they do these things in a green tree, what shall be done when the tree is dry?"

When they finally reached Golgotha, the place of the Skull, they offered Him wine mixed with myrrh and gall to deaden the pain of the crucifixion, but when He tasted it he refused to drink it. The soldiers drove the nails through the hands and feet of Christ, as well as the two evildoers with Him. They raised Him up, now attached to the cross, which they dropped into the hole that had been dug to keep it in place. They did the same to the two thieves, placing one on His right, and the other on His left.

When the chief priests had heard that the charge which was to be placed on the Cross above the head of Jesus was to say, "This is Jesus of Nazareth, the King of the Jews," they tried to persuade the Governor to change it.

They said, "Write, 'that man said I am King of the Jews.'"

Pilate said, "What I have written, I have written."

So at nine o'clock that morning, as the Lord hung suspended from the Cross, that charge written in Hebrew, Latin, and Greek was attached. And since the crucifixion site was near the city, many Jews saw it.

The soldiers who had followed with Jesus that morning took His belongings and divided them into four parts, and then cast lots to decide who would get which part. This left only His coat, which was woven from the top throughout with no seam.

They said to each other, "Let's not tear it, but let's cast lots for this also, to decide who gets it."

Then for the first time, the voice of Jesus was heard from the Cross, "Father, forgive them, for they don't know what they are doing."

As the soldiers sat down to keep watch over Jesus, it began. With His body beaten and bloody, nails driven through His hands, and a spike through His feet, the mocking began.

As some stood watching, others walked by wagging their heads, saying, "You Who destroy the Temple, and build it in three days, save Yourself. If you are the Son of God, come down from the Cross."

The chief priests, scribes, and elders joined in.

"He saved others, but He can't save Himself. Let the Christ, the King of Israel, come down now from the Cross, and then we'll believe in Him. He placed His trust in God. Let Him rescue Him now if He wants Him, since He said He was the Son of God."

The soldiers, who were able to come closer to Him than anyone else, mockingly offered Him vinegar to drink, and said, "If you're the King of the Jews, save yourself."

One of the thieves who was with Him added, "Yes, Aren't you supposed to be the Christ? Save yourself, and us, while you're at it."

The other condemned criminal who had also been ridiculing Him at first, now said to the other, "Don't you even fear God, since you're condemned to the same death. We deserve to be punished because of what we did, but this man has done nothing wrong."

This man then said to Jesus, "Lord, remember me when you come into Your kingdom."

Jesus said, "I assure you, today you will be with Me in Paradise."

Then He looked down on those who stood by His Cross- His mother, His mother's sister, Mary the wife of Cleopas, and Mary Magdalene. When He saw His mother, the Apostle John was standing with her.

He said to His mother, "Woman, behold your son."

Then He said to His Apostle, "Son, behold your mother."

The morning and mocking wore on, the light of the sun began to fail, and by noon the entire land was as dark as night. The darkness remained until three o'clock, when Jesus cried out, "Eloi, eloi, lama sabachthani."

What Jesus said was Hebrew for, "My God, My God, why have You forsaken Me," but some who stood nearby misunderstood what He said, and thought that He was actually calling on Elijah for help.

Shortly after this, Jesus said, "I'm thirsty."

Nearby was a container filled with sour wine. One of the soldiers ran and filled a sponge, and put it on a reed of hyssop to give Him a drink.

But the rest said, "Leave Him alone. Let's see whether Elijah comes to save Him."

After the man gave Him some of the wine, Jesus said, "It is finished."

Then He cried out with a loud voice, "Father, into Your hands I entrust My spirit."

He then bowed His head, and dismissed His spirit. At that moment there was an earthquake that shook the ground, splitting the large rocks into pieces, and opening the tombs of some of the saints.

In the Temple the veil, which was 60 feet long and 30 feet wide, was torn in two from top to bottom.

When the centurion and the others who were guarding Jesus saw the earthquake and the other things that happened, they said, "This truly was the Son of God."

All the people who had gathered to watch the Crucifixion began to walk back toward the city, beating their breasts from grief. A small group of women remained. Mary Magdalene, Mary the mother of James the Less and Joses, and Salome had followed with Jesus from Galilee, and had provided Him with the necessities of life. They had travelled with Him to Jerusalem, and had now witnessed this horrific event. Since this was the preparation for Passover, which was a very important Sabbath, the Jews didn't want the bodies of the three victims left on the crosses. Since they knew that it was forbidden for the men to be removed while still alive, they asked Pilate to have their legs broken, which would cause the end to come more quickly.

So the soldiers came to the first thief, and swung a heavy club which broke his legs; and then went to the other thief and did the same, causing them both to suffocate. But when they came to Jesus, they found Him already dead, so they didn't break His legs. Instead, a soldier took a spear and thrust it deeply into His side, causing blood and water to flow out.

*   *   *

When evening came, Joseph of Arimathea, a rich and honorable member of the Sanhedrin, dared to go see Pilate. He himself had not consented to the counsel or the actions of the other members of the Sanhedrin, and was actually a follower of Jesus, but had kept it a secret because he feared the Jews. But now he gathered his courage and boldly went to the governor, and asked him for the body of the Lord. Pilate wondered whether He was already dead, so he sent a messenger to the centurion to make sure it was true. When the officer verified that He had indeed died, he commanded that the body be given to Joseph.

Joseph went back to Golgotha with a piece of fine linen which he had bought and was met there by Nicodemus, also previously a secret disciple, who brought 100 hundred pounds of a mixture of myrrh and aloes.

They took down the body of the Lord and wound it in the linen cloth, and because the Sabbath was soon approaching, they took Him to a tomb located in a garden near where He was crucified. It belonged to Joseph, who had had the sepulcher cut out of rock, and it had never been used. When they entered the burial place, they laid the body on the low bench which was carved around the inside walls, where they anointed the body with spices and perfumes.

Mary Magdalene and Mary the mother of Joses sat watching as the men worked quickly. They had accompanied them so that they would know where He had been laid. Before they left the tomb, they rolled a great stone against the door.

*   *   *

The next day the chief priests and Pharisees met with Pontius Pilate, and said, "Sir, it occurred to us that while that deceiver was still alive, he said that after three days, He would be raised. Command that the tomb be made secure until the third day. This is just in case His disciples come, steal the body, and say to the people, 'He is risen from the dead.' It's bad enough that the people think He is the Messiah, but it would be even worse if they thought He was raised from the dead."

He said, "I'll give you a guard detail. Be on your way, and make it as secure as you know how."

They went to the tomb, and placed the seal of the Roman Empire on the stone, and the soldiers who witnessed it were left there to guard it.

In the meanwhile, after the Sabbath had ended, Mary Magdalene, Mary the mother of James the Less, and Salome bought sweet spices, which they prepared, so that the next morning they could return to the sepulcher to finish anointing the body of Jesus.

CHAPTER 40

The soldiers had been guarding the tomb since sunset on Friday. They had been ordered to remain here at this place for three days, because apparently the man buried here said He would rise from the dead on the third day, and obviously someone believed it. So here they sat in the darkness, waiting for sunrise, and looking forward to being free of all this. Suddenly the ground began to shake, and the stone in front of the tomb began to move. The men instantly jumped to their feet with weapons in hand, prepared for whatever was coming now. As the stone rolled away, these Roman soldiers came face to face with an angel who looked like a bolt of lightning clothed in glistening white. They trembled uncontrollably with fright, and then fainted. When they finally come to, they saw that the stone truly was removed, and the angel gone. Unfortunately, so was the man who had been buried there, and so they fled.

*   *   *

Now that the Sabbath was past, Mary Magdalene, Mary the mother of James, and Salome made their way through the darkness toward the place where Jesus was buried. They walked with downcast eyes, carrying the sweet spices they had bought, and prepared to finish anointing the body of Jesus.

The main question that kept going back and forth was, "Who will roll the stone away from the door of the tomb for us?"

But when they arrived at the burial place, they looked up and found that the huge stone had obviously been rolled away, and there was no sign of the guards. They entered into the now easily accessible tomb and were stunned to see two young men, dressed in white garments, who flashed like lightning. Fear stricken, they bowed their heads to the ground.

The men said, "Don't be afraid. Why are you looking for the living among the dead? You are looking for Jesus of Nazareth, the One Who was crucified. He's not here. He is risen. Look at the place where He was laid. Don't you remember what He told you while He was still with you in Galilee? He said, 'The Son of man must be delivered into the hands of sinful men, and be crucified, and the third day rise again.' Go on your way, and tell His disciples and Peter that He is going before them into Galilee: and they'll see Him there, just like He said."

They quickly fled from the tomb, trembling, and yet full of joy. They were in such a rush that they didn't stop and talk to anyone.

Then suddenly they came face to face with Jesus Himself, and He said, "All hail."

The women prostrated themselves on the ground in worship, and took hold of His feet.

He said, "Don't be afraid. Go and tell My brethren to go to Galilee, and they'll see me there."

When the women finally arrived to bring the news to the eleven, they found them mourning and weeping. When they told what had happened at the tomb, the men thought it sounded like nothing but nonsense, and they refused to believe them.

But then Mary Magdalene said, "The Lord has been taken from the tomb, and we don't know where they have taken Him."

Peter and John immediately set out running toward the tomb. John outran Peter and arrived there first. He stopped at the entrance to the sepulcher and looked in, and saw the strips of linen cloth lying there. When Peter arrived, he rushed by the other Apostle, directly into the tomb. As he stood looking around, he also saw the linen lying there, but he noticed the handkerchief that had been wrapped around the head of Jesus rolled up, and in a place by itself. After seeing Peter boldly go in, John also entered, saw, and believed. Finally they left, and returned to their homes.

Mary Magdalene had arrived while the two Apostles were examining the burial place, and remained there as the men left. She stood facing the tomb and wept. After a while, she gathered the courage to take a look inside for herself. She stooped down, peaked in, and saw two angels sitting where the body of Jesus had laid- one at the head, and the other at the foot.

They asked, "Woman, why are you weeping?"

She said, "Because they took away my Lord, and I don't know where they laid Him."

She then turned and saw Jesus, but was so full of grief and tears that she didn't recognize Him, and thought He was the gardener.

Jesus asked, "Woman, why are you weeping?"

She said, "Sir, if you carried Him off, please tell me where you laid Him, and I will take Him away."

Jesus then simply said, "Mary."

When she heard the familiar voice say her name, she turned, saw Him, and said, "Rabboni, my Master."

She grabbed Him, and clung tightly to Him, but He said, "You need to let Me go, for I haven't yet ascended to My Father. But go and tell My brethren, 'I am ascending to My Father, and your Father; to My God, and your God.'"

She went and found the disciples, and ran up to them.

"I have seen the Lord with my own eyes!"

She then shared with them what He had told her to tell them.

*   *   *

Some of the guards who had fled from the tomb came to see the chief priests, and gave them a report of all that had occurred that morning. All the elders gathered to discuss the situation.

After the conference, the soldiers were called in and told, "If anyone asks you what happened to the body of Jesus of Nazareth, you just tell them, 'His disciples came at night, and secretly took Him away while we were asleep.' If the governor should hear about this and want to punish you for letting this happen, don't worry. We'll talk to him, and make sure you don't get in trouble."

They gave the men enough money to encourage them to keep their promise. So they took the bribe, and did exactly what they were told.

*   *   *

Later that afternoon, Cleopas and another disciple walked on the road to Emmaus, a village seven miles away. They were in a heated conversation about all that had happened that day. As they were discussing and questioning one another, Jesus joined up with them on their journey, but they were kept from recognizing Him.

Jesus asked, "What are you men talking about?"

They came to a standstill, and in their gloominess said, "You must just be a visitor to Jerusalem if you don't know about the things that have happened here in the last few days."

He asked, "What things?"

"The things concerning Jesus of Nazareth, a prophet Who was mighty in word and deed in the sight of God and all the people: and how the chief priests and our rulers delivered Him up to be condemned to death, and crucified Him. But we hoped that He was the One Who would liberate Israel. Besides all this, it's now the third day since all these things happened. And also, some of our women amazed us when they came from the tomb early this morning, where they had gone to anoint His body. They said they hadn't found Him, but instead had seen angels that told them He was alive. Some of our other men went to the tomb, and found things just as the women said: but they didn't see Him."

Jesus said, "O dull of perception, and slow of heart to believe in all the things that the prophets spoke. Wasn't it necessary for the Christ to suffer these things, and to enter His glory?"

Beginning from Moses and all the Prophets, He interpreted to them in one Scripture passage after another concerning Himself. As they drew near to the village where the men were going, Jesus set out to continue His journey. But the men begged Him to spend the night there.

They said, "Be our guest: because it's late in the day, and it will be dark soon."

Later that night as they were sitting enjoying dinner, Jesus took the bread, and broke it. As He was giving it out, their eyes were opened, and they recognized Him; and He vanished before their eyes.

They said to one another, "Wasn't our heart burning within us as He talked with us along the road, and opened the Scriptures?"

They left that very hour and returned to Jerusalem.

They found the Apostles gathered together with some others, where they were told, "The Lord has truly risen, and appeared to Simon."

Then Cleopas and his companion rehearsed the things that happened on the road, and how He was made known to them by the breaking of the bread.

As they sat at the table with doors shut, out of fear of the Jews, Jesus Himself stepped out of nowhere into the midst of them, and said, "Peace be to you."

They were terrified and frightened, and thought they were seeing a spirit.

He said to them, "Why are you troubled, and why are these kinds of thoughts arising in your hearts? Look at My hands and My feet, and see for yourselves that it's Me. Touch Me and see; for a spirit doesn't have flesh and bones, as you see that I have."

He showed them His hands and His feet, as well as His side. They still doubted, because it seemed too good to be true; and so He said, "Do you have anything to eat?"

They gave Him a piece of broiled fish, and honeycomb; which He took and ate before them. Then the disciples were glad, when they saw that it truly was the Lord.

He said again, "Peace be to you. Just as the Father sent Me on a mission, I also am sending you."

When He said this, He breathed on them, and said, "Receive now the Holy Spirit. If you forgive the sins of any, they are forgiven; and if you retain anyone's sins, they remain unforgiven."

After Jesus left, Thomas, the only one of the Apostles who was missing, returned. The other disciples said, "We have seen the Lord with our own eyes."

He said, "If I don't see the mark of the nails in His hands, and put my finger into the print of the nails, and thrust my hand into His side, there is no way I would believe that."

*   *   *

Eight days later the disciples were again in the Upper Room, with the doors tightly closed: and this time Thomas was there when Jesus came. As He again stood in the midst of them, He spoke to Thomas.

"Come here and reach out your finger, and look at My hands. Reach out your hand, and thrust it into My side: and don't be faithless, but believing."

Thomas confessed, "My Lord and my God."

Jesus said, "You have believed, because you've now seen: but the ones who are truly blessed are those who have not seen, and yet believe."

CHAPTER 41

Sometime after, Jesus appeared to His disciples a third time. Peter, Thomas, Nathanael, the sons of Zebedee, and two other disciples were together in a boat on the Sea of Tiberias. Peter had announced that he was going to go fishing, and the others agreed to join him. They spent all night fishing, but failed to catch anything. As day began to break, Jesus stood on the beach: but the men on the boat didn't recognize Him in the dim morning light.

He called out, "Boys, you don't have any fish, do you?"

They answered, "No."

So He said, "Throw the net on the right side of the boat, and you'll find some."

When they cast it into the water on the right side, it became so full of fish that, as much as they struggled with it, they couldn't draw the net onto the boat, because it was so heavy.

John said to Peter, "It's the Lord."

When Peter heard this, he wrapped his fisher's coat around

himself, and threw himself into the sea, and began to swim to shore. The other disciples finally brought the little boat the three hundred feet to shore, dragging the net full of fish.

As soon as they got off the boat onto the beach, they saw fish cooking on a charcoal fire, along with some bread.

Jesus said, "Bring some of the fish you caught."

Peter went up into the boat and drew the net onto the land. It was full of 153 great fish: and he saw that in spite of the massive catch, the net had not split.

Jesus called to them, "Come have some breakfast."

None of the disciples dared to ask Him, 'Who are You?' because they knew it was the Lord. Jesus came and served them the bread and fish.

After they had eaten, Jesus asked Simon Peter, "Simon, son of Jonas, do you love Me more than these other men?"

"Yes, Lord. You know that I love you."

"Feed My lambs."

Jesus then asked a second time, "Simon, son of Jonas, do you love Me?"

"Yes, Lord. You know that I love you."

"Feed My sheep."

Then a third time Jesus asked, "Simon, son of Jonas, do you love Me?"

Peter was upset when he heard Jesus ask him the third time, "Do you love Me?"

He replied, "Lord, You know everything, so you know that I love you."

Jesus said, "Feed My sheep. I assure you, when you were younger, you would clothe yourself as you wanted, and walk around freely where you wanted to go. But when you get older, you'll stretch out your hands, and another shall bind you up, and carry you where you don't want to go. Follow Me."

As they got up to leave, Peter suddenly turned around, and when he saw John, he asked, "Lord, what about him?"

Jesus answered, "If I want him to remain till I come, that

doesn't concern you. You just continue following Me."

*   *   *

Another day, the eleven disciples went to Galilee to a mountain where they were to meet Jesus. And when they saw Him approaching, they bowed themselves down in worship. When Jesus reached them, He said, "All authority is given to Me in Heaven and on earth. Go into all the world, and preach the Gospel to all of creation. The one who believes and is baptized will be saved; but the one who does not believe shall be condemned. Along with this, teach and make disciples of all nations, baptizing them in the Name of the Father, and of the Son, and of the Holy Spirit.

Teach them to observe and hold firmly to whatever I have commanded you. And these signs shall accompany those who believe; In My Name they shall cast out demons; they shall speak with new tongues; they shall pick up snakes; and if they drink any deadly thing, it will not hurt them; they shall lay hands on the sick, and they shall recover. And, behold, I Myself will always be with you, even till the end of the world."

*   *   *

Once again Jesus appeared to His disciples when they were in Jerusalem. He said, "These are the words which I spoke to you, while I was still with you, that it was necessary for all the things which were written in the Law of Moses, and in the Prophets, and in the Psalms, concerning Me to be fulfilled."

Then He opened their minds, so that they might understand the Scriptures; and said to them, "Thus it is written, that the Christ should suffer, and rise from the dead on the third day: and that there is repentance and the remission of sins in His Name, to be preached to all nations, beginning at Jerusalem. You are the ones who have seen these things take place, so you must testify about them. And, behold, I am sending forth the promise of My Father upon you. Stay in the city of Jerusalem, until you are clothed with power from on high."

*   *   *

On the 40th day since His resurrection, Jesus led a crowd of His disciples out of Jerusalem up towards the road to Bethany. They continued on till they reached the ridge of the Mount of Olives, looking down on the Holy City. He lifted up His hands, and as He blessed them, He was parted from them, and began to ascend up on a cloud to Heaven, where He sat down on the right hand of God the Father.

The disciples worshipped Him, and afterwards returned to Jerusalem: and they were continually in the Temple, praising and blessing God. And they went forth as He had told them, and preached everywhere; and the Lord worked with them, confirming the Word with supernatural signs accompanying them.

EPILOGUE

There were many other things that Jesus did in the sight of the disciples which were not written in this book. If each one were written down, I don't suppose that the world itself could contain the books that would be written. But these have been written that you might believe that Jesus is the Christ, the Son of God, and that by believing you might have eternal life in His Name.

John, the Disciple whom Jesus loved